God's Economy

Ron McKenzie
Kingwatch Books

Kingwatch Books
Christchurch
New Zealand
www.kingwatch.co.nz

Contents

The Big Picture

God's Economy is the last in a series of five books that all fit together to tell God's plan for his people and his earth.

Being Church Where We Live explains how a group of people who have chosen to follow Jesus can support each other in a neighbourhood church by giving and sharing. By living close together, they will establish a place where the authority of Jesus is acknowledged and the spiritual powers of evil are squeezed out.

Each neighbourhood church will be led by a team of elders with complementary and balanced giftings: one will be prophetic, at least one will be an evangelist and several will have a shepherd gifting. They will be bound together by love and submitted to each other for spiritual protection. They will watch over those who have chosen to follow Jesus.

Neighbourhood churches grow and multiply by sending apostles into a new neighbourhood to establish a new community. These communities of love are the essential foundation that makes possible everything described in subsequent books.

Kingdom Authority describes God's plan for getting back the authority lost to the spiritual powers of evil and establishing his Kingdom on earth. Human politics are an obstacle to the Kingdom of God because they use Imposed Authority which empowers the powers of evil. Government-spirits have leveraged their feeble power by controlling political and military authorities. In contrast, God refuses to impose his authority on earth using force and coercion. He rejects all forms of political and military power. Instead, he calls people to serve him and freely submit to his will because they love Jesus. This is Free Authority.

Times and Seasons describes how human governments seize more and more power to deal with the economic and social crises that their mistakes have created. They will collapse under the weight of their pride and hubris, which will provide an opportunity for God's people who are prepared. During a season of distress, they will work with the Holy Spirit to proclaim the gospel and bring in the Kingdom of God.

Government of God explains the perfect system of government that God gave through Moses when he was leading the children of Israel into the promised land. This alternative system of justice, welfare and defence relies on Free Authority. It does not need the coercion and force of Imposed Authority. The book describes how God's people can prepare for the collapse of human government by applying these principles within Kingdom Communities.

A neighbourhood church becomes a Kingdom Community by providing everyone living in their neighbourhood with the services that governments promise, but fail to deliver. They will provide social support, justice and protection for everyone in their neighbourhood, regardless of whether they have chosen to follow Jesus. When people submit to the wisdom of the elders of a Kingdom Community to obtain these benefits, they are part of the Kingdom of God even though they have not chosen to follow Jesus.

The Kingdom of God is the goal of everything, but there are no kingdoms left on earth, so the word "kingdom" is not very helpful to modern people. The best way to understand the nature of a kingdom is to think of it as a "government", so I often refer to it as the "Government of God" to make its role and nature clear. This explains the title of this book.

God's Economy is the final book in this series. Everything on earth belongs to God, so all our economic activity is part of his economy, whether we acknowledge him or not. This book describes the Instructions for Economic Life that God gave through Moses. Jesus confirmed this guidance and adapted it for people who are loving one another in a Kingdom Community.

All economic and business activity is part of God's Economy. Applying the Instructions for Economic Life will completely transform our economic behaviour and business activity.

Note

God's Economy will be easier to understand if ***Being Church Where We Live*** and ***Government of God*** have been read first. God's Economy needs local judges applying God's law to deal with theft and dishonesty in the way described in Government of God

Book Outline

God's Economy has three parts.

Part One describes God's Instructions for Economic Life. Jesus confirmed these instructions and adapted them to work in a society in which tribal connections have broken down. He explained how they apply to the communities of love that he was establishing amongst the people who chose to follow him. He shifted the focus from neighbours to people who are committed to loving one another, but the core principles are the same.

Part Two applies God's Instructions for Economic Life to modern society. God does not expect the people of the world to live according to these instructions, but he requires those who have chosen to serve Jesus to apply his wisdom in their lives and communities.

These instructions are only practical amongst people who are being the church where they live. They can apply God's instructions without relying on government enforcement while continuing to live in a world that is dominated by the existing power systems. God's economy will become a witness and sign to a world that has lost its way.

The first two chapters of **Part Three** describe the problems with modern money and banking. These flaws inevitably produce economic instability, inequality and often extreme poverty. Followers of Jesus need to understand these problems, but they do not prevent them from living out God's Instructions for Economic Life within their Kingdom Communities.

The last three chapters of Part 3 explain how better money and financial institutions can be established within their Kingdom Communities in preparation for the time when the kingdoms of the world collapse and fall.

Getting everything that needs to be in a book about the God's Economy is almost impossible. I have concentrated on economic ideas that are new and different, rather than trying to cover everything that might be relevant. I focus on the changes that are necessary for the emergence of the Government of God.

Preface

I grew up on a farm, so I left school early to work in farming. After a couple of years, I realised that I did not have the strength and stamina that farming needs, so I decided to go to university. While working with sheep and driving the tractor, I had plenty of time to think about the poverty and suffering that were rampant throughout the world. The problems seemed to be economic and political, so I enrolled to study economics and politics.

After four years of study, I realised that I was digging a dry well. The assumptions that economists have to make to ensure their models work are so unrealistic that their theories are irrelevant to the real world. It seemed that during the first three years of economics, they told you all the solutions, but in the fourth year, they explained why they would not work. (I noted that my fellow students who went into politics, often only did the three-year course, so they went out boldly assuming they had effective policies).

While growing up, our family had gone to church every Sunday, but for me, it was just a habit. When I reached university and encountered modern philosophy, I gave up my religious habit. However, just when I became disillusioned with economics, I heard the gospel of Jesus clearly for the first time. I surrendered to him and committed to living by his word and Spirit.

A few months later, I had an exam for a post-graduate course on comparative economics. The lecturer was a staunch Marxist. Full of my new-found faith, I wrote in my paper that Marx has no solution to human problems and that Jesus is the answer. I gave a similar response in a paper on macroeconomics.

Surprisingly, I passed the course with first class honours. However, at the beginning of the following year, one of my professors asked to meet with me. He disclosed that he was an atheist, but acknowledged that my faith seemed to be genuine. He told me that it was not enough to say that Jesus is the answer. I needed to explain how he could be a solution to the problems that concerned me. He concluded with a telling question: "What would the economy and society look like if everyone was a Christian".

I could not answer his question, but I knew that I had to find the answer to it. I did not know enough about God, or his solutions to economic problems, but I made it my goal to find out.

I went to seminary for three years and studied theology and New Testament Greek. Later I studied Hebrew for two years to get a better understanding of the Old Testament. While employed as an economist, I read every book and article that I could find that is relevant to economics and the gospel.

Economics and Politics

About ten years ago, I felt that I was ready to answer the question that my atheist teacher had asked, but one more obstacle lay in the way. I still had faith in political power. I believed that God's people could use political power to establish his Kingdom on earth. I needed to grasp the failures and futility of politics.

Modern economics is mostly politics. The solutions dreamt up by economists can only be implemented by a government with coercive power, so economics becomes a servant of politics.

- Fiscal policy explains why politicians should take money from some people and use it to benefit others.
- Monetary policy explains how governments can control the creation of money and who should benefit.

- Labour economics guides politicians who want to control employment practices and pay.

Modern economics and politics are hard to separate. Economic principles get caught up in political power.

Jesus refused to use political power to advance the Kingdom of God (Luke 22:25-26; John 18:36). Political spirits and government spirits have used political authority to leverage their power on earth. Evil cannot be used to accomplish good.

When I studied this issue seriously, I discovered that God had already given a system of government to Moses that does not rely on force and coercion. I described his system of local judges applying his law and voluntary military leaders protecting their community in a book called Government of God (2017). It explains how Kingdom Communities can function without political power. They can voluntarily provide all the services that human governments promise, but fail to deliver.

Once I understood the problems of political power, my understanding of the nature of economics changed dramatically. The policies of modern economists cannot enter the Kingdom of God because they need to be imposed from the top by human governments with the power to make people do the right thing. I began seeking a politics-free economics.

I discovered the Instructions for Economic Life that God gave to Moses (see chapter 2). I also found that Jesus had validated these instructions in his teaching about economics (see chapter 3). God's instructions allow a community of people to develop an economy that can function effectively without the need for political power and coercion.

The advance of the gospel by the power of the Spirit should produce a radically different economy. The most significant change is that there will be no human government to enforce economic policies. Economic change will come as more and more people choose to follow Jesus and are prompted by the Holy Spirit to obey his commands.

God's economy is not modern capitalism. Modern capitalism is a system in which all activities are commercialised. Big businesses collude with political power to gain wealth at the expense of ordinary people. Materialism and consumerism are advanced at the expense of relationships. The strong are rewarded, the weak suffer. God's economy is radically different from modern capitalism.

This book describes the changes to economic activity that will occur as the Government of God comes to fullness. It seeks to answer the following question: "What would an economy look like if most people chose to follow Jesus and the Holy Spirit was able to establish the Government of God?". This is the question my economics teacher asked me back in 1975.

As the gospel advances, followers of Jesus will form Kingdom Communities that implement his system of justice, protection and welfare (as described in Government of God).   God's economy will emerge as these communities apply Jesus' interpretation of the Instructions for Economic Life.

The practical outworking of God's economic wisdom will vary according to local cultural and living arrangements. People will have to work out the details by following the leading of the Holy Spirit and adapting the principles to their local situation.

1

Good Economics

No Values

Modern economics has no values. Modern economists do not do morality. Instead, they prefer to study how economies work, without making any value judgments about what they discover. Their ideal economic system is the one that functions best.

Secular economists have no absolute ethical standards to determine what is good or bad. They have left politicians to decide what should be done, while they concentrated on working out how political goals could be achieved.

This avoidance of ethical issues has been an embarrassment. An economist who cannot tell you what should be done is not much help, so in recent years, economists have sneaked ethics back into their discipline. One approach has been to use cost-benefit analysis. An economic program is good if the social benefit exceeds the social costs. The impossibility of measuring social costs and social benefits is conveniently ignored.

More recently, efficiency has become the highest good. Economists do studies to decide which level of tax is most efficient, in terms of gathering the most revenue for the least loss of production. Once the most efficient tax rate has been decided, it suddenly becomes something that should be implemented. Efficient morphs into ethical.

God's Economy

Most economists are pragmatic. They ask what will work. What will produce the desired outcome? What policies will generate economic growth? Which economic system is the most efficient? What policies will increase income and wealth?

I take the opposite approach. I am not interested in finding out what works. I am not interested in the system that produces the most wealth. My focus is on what is morally right and good. God's people should pursue what is good, even if it is not perfectly efficient, or the best way of doing things. We should do what is right, even if it results in declining income and wealth.

God's economy is a good economy. Since we have his ethical standards, we can describe how a good economy would function. What will produce the most wealth is not relevant. What matters for a follower of Jesus is obeying him. We want an economy that is right and good in his eyes, even if it does not function as well as other systems. It is better to be good before God than to be prosperous or wealthy.

Economic activity is interconnected, so most economic problems produce multiple symptoms. I try not to be distracted by symptoms and do not try to describe them all. Instead, I attempt to dig down to the underlying moral cause. A solution to these moral problems will eliminate the various symptoms.

I see most economic issues as ethical questions: what should be done, not what will work. Our question about every economic policy should be this: Is it morally right? Does it comply with God's word? Is it good?

A good economic policy is one that complies with God's ethical standards. The irony is that the right economic policies may not achieve the goals that many politician's desire: fast economic growth or equal income distribution. However, Christians should always be advocates for the right policies, not effective policies.

In the long term, obedience to God will lead to blessings, so everything will be fine, but in the short-term, the right economic policies may make some people worse off. However, they are still the right policies, because God's way is the best way.

Three Word Version

Good economics can be expressed in three words (two in Hebrew).

Do not steal (Ex 20:15).

This is one of two universal laws that God gave through Moses. It is God's most important standard for economic behaviour. If an economic policy or practice involves stealing it is wrong.

When investigating an economic problem, I ignore the symptoms and dig down to find the place where theft has occurred. This approach usually exposes the cause of economic problems, as they are mostly the result of a theft of some kind.

Most of the economic teaching in the Old Testament is an application of the command prohibiting theft. Jesus' teaching about economic activity affirmed this principle. He described money that had been stolen as unrighteous wealth (Unrighteous wealth is covered in chapter 4.)

Five Word Version

God's economics can also be expressed in five words.

Love your neighbour as yourself (Lev 19:18).

The command was originally given by Moses as part of his instructions to the children of Israel. Jesus used this command as the heart of his teaching about economics. He said this is the second-greatest command, after loving God.

Love your neighbour as yourself (Luke 10:27).

James repeated the same command in his letter (James 2:8).

The five-word version turns the three-word version positive. If we love people, we will not be able to steal from them. Love can guide all economic actions in the community in which we live.

Jesus expanded the definition of our neighbour to include everyone whom we have contact with during everyday life (Luke 10:25-37). This means that our neighbour is not just those we like, or those living close by. Our neighbour is everyone we encounter while engaged in economic activity. It includes those we buy from and sell to, as well as those we employ.

Jesus set a higher standard for his followers than Moses. Loving neighbours is much harder than not stealing. Only those who walk in the Holy Spirit are expected to do it. People who have not accepted the gospel and the Spirit just have to comply with the standard of the law, which is "do not steal". Followers of Jesus have a higher standard. All their encounters with people during economic activity must be governed by Jesus' command to love your neighbour as yourself (This is described more fully in chapter 2 and 3).

Holding back the Curse

The primary role of modern economists is to advise governments. They attempt to develop policies that will improve the performance of the economy in their nation. They seek policies that will be optimal for their society.

The problem with this objective is that a nation that has forgotten God is under a curse. The scriptures promise blessings for people who honour and trust God. These blessings are social and economic, so serving him will bring social and economic blessings.

When the people of a nation or city reject God, they lose the blessing that comes from following him. The best solution is to turn back to God, but people often do not want to do that. To avoid returning to God, people look for other ways to escape the curse. The most popular solution is electing governments who promise to make things better, despite the curse. Most people believe that their government will save them from the problems that plague their society and economy.

Economists support governments in this role by offering economic policies that will deal with the problems that disobedience is creating. Unfortunately, all attempts to hold back the curse will fail. God's way is best, so ignoring him has a cost. Therefore, when human governments solve one economic problem, another economic or social problem pops out in its place.

During the 1950s and 60s, economists believed that they had economic policies that would prevent economic depressions. However, their solutions produced rampant inflation, which robbed people on fixed incomes and created stagnant economies. The economic policies developed to solve the inflation problem eventually produced the Global Financial Crisis in 2007. Resolving one consequence of the curse just releases it in a different form.

In a world full of sinful people, economic disruption and depression will be common and persistent, so economic policies developed to resolve the curse will usually fail. When economists come up with a solution to one aspect of the curse, they usually empower another manifestation of it.

No Government

The consequence of sin is that attempts by governments to create a better world always fail. Under the Government of God, there is no place for human governments, such as kings, presidents and Prime Minister. When the children of Israel were entering the promised land, God gave Moses his guidance for human families and communities to live together in a peaceful society and strong economy. These instructions have no role for kings or governments.

God provided a system of law that prohibited crimes like theft and assault, which would disrupt society. He also provided a system of local judges to implement these laws and apply the specified penalties for these crimes. These judges dealt with theft by specifying restitution (Ex 22:1). God also provided a system of defence that relies on local militias and temporary military leaders, so a king with a large standing army is not needed.

God's system of justice and defence does not need kings and governments. Justice is administered in local communities by local judges. God has provided his laws, so a parliament is not required to make laws.

I have described how this radically different approach to government can function in a book called Government of God. You will need to read that book to understand the teaching contained in this one. Government of God focuses on the law, justice, crime and defence. This book covers economic aspects of the Kingdom of God that are not covered in that book.

If I am correct that there is no role for modern governments in the Kingdom of God, then the role of economics changes dramatically. It is pointless developing economic policies for governments to implement if there are no governments. This limits the role of economists to understanding how economies function, without any attempt to develop government policies to make them perform better.

Different Objective

The proclamation of the gospel and the moving of the Holy Spirit will radically change the way that an economy operates. It will be very different from both the globalised capitalist economy and the socialist economies that prevail in many countries now.

In the world system, the main goal is increasing income and wealth. There are debates about how equal the income distribution should be, but the overall goal is to maximise income and wealth. Economic policies are assessed against their ability to increase production and consumption of goods and services.

In the Kingdom economy, obedience to God's standards is more important than increasing income and wealth. Doing what is right is more important than increasing prosperity. Discovering economic policies that align with God's word will be the goal.

Jesus on Economics

Throughout his ministry on earth, Jesus spoke strongly and clearly about economic issues. However, most of his teaching about economics was confirmation and explanation of the Instructions for Economic Life that God had given to Moses. So before investigating Jesus' teaching on economic life in chapter 3, I will analyse Moses' Instructions for Economic Life in chapter 2.

Part 1

Instructions for Economic Life

Part One describes God's Instructions for Economic Life. Jesus confirmed these instructions and adapted them to work in a society in which tribal connections have broken down. He explained how they apply to the communities of love that he was establishing amongst the people who chose to follow him. He shifted the focus from neighbours to people who are committed to loving one another, but the core principles are the same.

2

Instructions for Economic Life

Most Christians ignore God's law because they see it as the opposite of grace. Jesus had a different view.

> Do not think that I have come to abolish the Law or the Prophets; I have not come to abolish them but to fulfil them. For truly I tell you, until heaven and earth disappear, not the smallest letter, not the least stroke of a pen, will by any means disappear from the Law until everything is accomplished (Matt 5:17-18).

If Jesus intends us to practice these commands, we need to know more about them. David agreed with Jesus.

> Oh, how I love your law!
> I meditate on it all day long.
> Your commands are always with me
> and make me wiser than my enemies.
> I have more insight than all my teachers,
> for I meditate on your statutes.
> I have more understanding than the elders,
> for I obey your precepts (Psalm 119:97-100).

If loving the law can make a person wise, we need to understand more about what it teaches.

Guidance for Communities

The law is not 600 rules that we must keep to please God. The Hebrew name for the law is Torah, which means "teaching". It contains the teaching of God on many aspects of human life, including social and economic guidance to enable a community of people to live together in harmony.

God gave Israel a radically different system of justice and economic life that do not require centralised government powers. The Israelites had a decentralised society, where households and families lived close to each other within tribal groupings. The law of Moses also provided guidelines for groups of people to live peacefully together in a community without government control.

Most of the interaction between households and communities was economic, so the Torah contained guidance about their economic activity. I call this wisdom "Instructions for Economic Life". These were not formal laws, but voluntary instructions to guide the economic behaviour of the people. The Instructions for Economic Life made it easier for them to live together in peace in a decentralised society. God promised great blessing for those who applied these principles to their economic life (Deut 28).

Love the Law

The Instructions for Economic life deal with poverty, debt, money, land, work and employment. These issues are still the concerns of economics.

The verses referenced in this chapter were not cherry-picked or pulled out randomly. Several years ago, I grasped the implications of Psalm 119 and learned to love the law. To assist my detailed study of the law, I copied all the laws and commands in Exodus, Leviticus, Numbers and Deuteronomy into a spreadsheet.

I set aside those that referred to the sacrifices and the priesthood because I assumed that they had been fulfilled in Jesus. This left me with about 250 commands that I grouped into nearly twenty-five categories. One of my main categories was "economic life". More than thirty commands fell into this group. I cover them systematically in this chapter (except for a few that are developed extensively in later chapters).

Love your Neighbour

A fundamental instruction underpins all the Instructions for Economic Life.

> Love your neighbour as yourself. I am the Lord (Lev 19:18).

This principle was not a radical invention by Jesus. It was right there in the heart of the Torah, given in Leviticus (a book that most Christians choose to ignore). This command is the basis for all the Instructions for Economic Life. The key to strong communities is people loving their neighbours as themselves.

The Instructions for Economic Life provide guidance to God's people for living together in a new land. His primary goal was that they learn to love their neighbours (Lev 19:18).

God is not a control freak. He wants his people to be free, so he did not give detailed regulations spelt out in black and white. Instead, he gave general principles and left the people to work out how to apply them by thinking about how they could love their neighbours.

The Pharisees wanted detailed rules, down to the level of which herbs to tithe on (Matt 23:23). But God is not interested in rule-based conformity, he wants love-motivated behaviour. Following detailed rules is often easier because it does not require thinking, but that was not what God wanted. He gave general instructions for economic conduct and left his people to work out want they meant while loving their neighbours.

This principle applies even more in the age of the Spirit. The Instructions for Economic Life are not detailed rules. They provide general boundaries, but our daily actions must be shaped by loving one another within their guidance (Rom 13:10). Likewise, the Holy Spirit does not give us detailed minute-by-minute instructions on what to do each day. He teaches us how to apply God's general Instructions for Economic Life as we attempt to love one another.

Care for Neighbours

Loving your neighbour means caring for their safety. Special care was an obligation to people who are disabled in some way.

> Do not curse the deaf or put a stumbling block in front of the blind, but fear your God. I am the Lord (Lev 19:14).

Every member of the community is obliged to ensure that disabled people do not come to harm.

People are expected to keep their buildings safe so that anyone entering their property would not be harmed.

> When you build a new house, make a parapet around your roof so that you may not bring the guilt of bloodshed on your house if someone falls from the roof (Deut 22:8).

This principle can be generalised to a variety of situations. Any activity that people undertake must be safe for their neighbours.

Businesses must design their warehouses and factories so that they do not harm their neighbours. Retailers must design their stores so that people who visit to shop are kept safe. Businesses cannot ignore the consequences of their actions. They are responsible for their neighbour's safety.

Care for Property

Every member of the community is required to look out for their neighbour's property and take care of it. If a person sees something belonging to a neighbour at risk, they must protect it.

> If you see someone's ox or sheep straying, do not ignore it but be sure to take it back to its owner. If they do not live near you or if you do not know who owns it, take it home with you and keep it until they come looking for it. Then give it back. Do the same if you find their donkey or cloak or anything else they have lost. Do not ignore it. If you see a donkey or ox fallen on the road, do not ignore it. Help the owner get it to its feet (Deut 22:1-4).

This requirement even applies to someone who dislikes us.

> If you come across your enemy's ox or donkey wandering off, be sure to return it. If you see the donkey of someone who hates you fallen down under its load, do not leave it there; be sure you help them with it (Ex 23:4-5).

Being kind to friends is easy. The Torah requires people to care for the property of their enemies. This means that people in business cannot just ignore something that would destroy their competitor's business. We have a duty of care for our enemies.

When Jesus challenged his listeners to love their enemies, he was not introducing a new concept. He was confirming that the command to love our neighbour applied to neighbours who hated us, not just those who love us.

Care for Nature

God's people are required to take care of the natural world.

> If you come across a bird's nest beside the road, either in a tree or on the ground, and the mother is sitting on the young or on the eggs, do not take the mother with the young. You may take the young, but be sure to let the mother go, so that it may go well with you and you may have a long life (Deut 22:6-7).

It is permissible to take a young bird or eggs for food, but the mother must be protected. This ensures that breeding and hatching will continue.

This principle can be generalised. God gave humans dominion over the earth. That does not mean that we can exploit it as we choose. We can use the products of the earth, including birds, animals and fruit. But we must ensure that enough breeding stock remains to preserve each species for future generations.

We are allowed to consume the product of the earth, but we must be careful not to harm God's world while doing it. Businesses must be careful not to push the costs of running their business onto their neighbours by failing to contain negative effects on their own property (Ex 22:6). They must not pollute their neighbour's air with fumes or their water with chemicals. They must not create excessive noise that would hurt their neighbours. Businesses that harm their neighbours have stolen from them, so they must put the situation right.

Conservation of nature is not a new idea. God put it in the Torah when he gave it to Moses. There are no specific penalties for failing to obey this command. However, there is a warning that if it is ignored, life on the land will not go well.

Care for Animals

In Moses time, oxen were used for threshing grain. When the wheat was cut, it was laid on an area of hard ground called the threshing floor. Oxen would be made to walk in a circle on the threshing floor and the pressure of the hooves would break the grain off the stalks of wheat. The next step took place on a windy day. The farm would toss the trampled wheat into the air with a winnowing fork. The wind would blow the chaff away while the grain would fall to the ground.

> Do not muzzle an ox while it is treading out the grain (Deut 25:4).

Animals can be used to provide mechanical power, but the owner must feed working animals really well. God's people must always be kind to animals.

Care for Employees

People employed to do work must be treated well.

> Do not take advantage of a hired worker who is poor and needy, whether that worker is a fellow Israelite or a foreigner residing in one of your towns. Pay them their wages each day before sunset, because they are poor and are counting on it. Otherwise, they may cry to the Lord against you, and you will be guilty of sin (Deut 24:14-15).

A person who needs to work for wages must be treated respectfully. This applies to both people living in the neighbourhood and foreigners who are there temporarily. The foreigner who becomes an employee is a neighbour. They must be loved as a neighbour.

A critical part of being a good neighbour is paying generous wages. God's people should not be satisfied with paying a legal minimum wage. He expects more than that. His people should pay all their employees sufficient for them to live on. An employee has no time left to produce their own food and shelter, so they need to be paid enough to buy it.

An employer should not just think about their own convenience but do what is best for their employee. If the person is destitute, they will not be able to wait until the end of the week for their money, because they would be without food. Even though it is inconvenient for the employer, a very poor person should be paid each day. They have done their work, so they are entitled to be paid. In the modern world, weekly or fortnightly pay has become the standard, but that makes life really hard for some people.

> Do not defraud or rob your neighbour. Do not hold back the wages of a hired worker overnight (Lev 19:13).

God's Instructions for Economic Life says that holding back the wages of a hired worker overnight is the same as defrauding them.

This command has general application. An employer must treat their employees in the same way as a neighbour. Employees should be paid promptly and generously.

Employers must ensure that their employees have sufficient to live on. This rules out zero-hours contracts and casual part-time contracts that commit people to being available for work but do not give them enough to live on. Employers must offer their employees enough work to allow them to earn sufficient to live on (Chapter 12 has more teaching about employment).

Honest Trade
All buying and selling must be done honestly.

> Do not have two differing weights in your bag—one heavy, one light. Do not have two differing measures in your house—one large, one small. You must have accurate and honest weights and measures, so that you may live long in the land the Lord your God is giving you. For the Lord your God detests anyone who does these things, anyone who deals dishonestly (Deut 25:13-16).

This command was given in a context where coins were not available for trade. Payments for purchases were made by weighing out gold or silver. A smart way to defraud people was to use light weights when making payments and a different set of heavier weights when getting paid.

The command applies to everyone who is selling goods or services. They must represent the stuff that they are selling accurately. Selling flawed goods as if they are good quality is wrong, because "God detests anyone who deals dishonestly". God's people should be known as honest traders. Two comments are common in business:

- Let the buyer beware.
- What the market will bear.

These phrases have no place amongst God's people.

The person with the scales has power. Most people dealing with them would have to trust their honesty because they could not afford their own scales. God gets upset when people with economic power use it dishonestly. (This command applies to all forms of money. Money and banking are covered in more detail in chapters 15-19).

No Coveting

For a community to be strong, people must be satisfied with what they have, even if others have more.

> You shall not covet your neighbour's house. You shall not covet your neighbour's wife, or his male or female servant, his ox or donkey, or anything that belongs to your neighbour (Ex 20:17, cf Deut 5:21).

This command has no penalty because coveting occurs in a person's heart, so there are no witnesses to testify against it. Coveting can tear a community apart. We must not look at any of the things that a person in our neighbourhood owns and wish that it were ours.

Modern advertising is based on persuading people to covet the things that a person who looks like their neighbour is flaunting. Activities that foster foolish coveting should be resisted because they are dangerous for a community.

Duty to the Poor

In any community, some people do well and others do badly. The Instructions for Economic Life provide safeguards for the poor.

> When you reap the harvest of your land, do not reap to the very edges of your field or gather the gleanings of your harvest. Do not go over your vineyard a second time or pick up the grapes that have fallen. Leave them for the poor and the foreigner. I am the Lord your God (Lev 19:9-10).

The people in a neighbourhood are to leave some of their crops for the poor to harvest (see also Deut 24:19-21). This is not a handout because the poor have to work to get the food.

This assistance is not just for immediate neighbours. It must be offered to foreigners who have chosen to live in the neighbourhood. Ruth was a Moabite, and Moab was an enemy of Israel, yet Boaz allowed her to glean in his fields.

Gleaning only works in agricultural societies, but the principle applies everywhere. God expects productive people to find ways to give some of what they have produced to the poor. Giving to relief organisations is not sufficient. God prefers that we bless the poor living in our neighbourhoods by developing modern equivalents of gleaning. Likewise, people in business must assist the people in their neighbourhood. More is expected from those who have been given much (Luke 12:48).

The gleaning command does not mean that poor people can reap other people's crops. A duty of care remains.

> If you enter your neighbour's vineyard, you may eat all the grapes you want, but do not put any in your basket. If you enter your neighbour's grainfield, you may pick kernels with your hands, but you must not put a sickle to their standing grain (Deut 23:24-25).

A hungry person walking past a vineyard can take a few grapes, but they are not to use a container. A person walking through a wheat field can take a few grains in their hands to quell their hunger, but they must not use a sickle to cut the grain.

Widows and Orphans

Widows and orphans suffer through no fault of their own.

> Do not take advantage of the widow or the fatherless. If you do and they cry out to me, I will certainly hear their cry (Ex 22:22-23).

Women whose husbands die young while their children are dependent are left in a vulnerable situation. They will have to earn enough to support their family, while not neglecting their children. Children who lose their parents while they are young are left in a helpless position. God expects the people in a neighbourhood to care for the widows and orphans living among them.

God is very serious about this obligation. He warned that a community that does not care for its orphans and widows brings judgment on itself. This is probably the cause of violence in many societies.

Loans to the Poor

If the situation of the poor person is not too severe, then someone in their neighbourhood should lend them money to enable them to get back on their feet again. Loans to the poor have two conditions.

1. A poor person must not be charged interest.

> If you lend money to one of my people among you who is poor,
> do not be like a moneylender; charge him no interest (Ex 22:25).

Interest is a killer for poor people because if they fail to pay it, the interest is added to the principal with penalties. A small loan can turn into a huge debt in a short time. Interest changes a loan from a blessing to a curse (Lev 25:35-37).

An interest-free loan may be enough to get some poor people going again. It gives them a strong incentive to work so that they can repay the loan. The ban on interest prevents their debt from growing unnecessarily, even if life continues to be tough.

2. A loan to a poor person that has not been repaid after seven years must be cancelled.

> At the end of every seven years you must cancel debts. This
> is how it is to be done: Every creditor shall cancel the loan he
> has made to his fellow Israelite. He shall not require payment
> from his fellow Israelite or brother, because the Lord's time
> for cancelling debts has been proclaimed (Deut 15:1-2).

The purpose of the loan is to help a poor person get back on their feet. If they fail to repay the loan, it must be wiped out after seven years. This prevents the loan from becoming a heavy burden for the person who cannot get on top of their debt.

Loans to the poor are really a gift that must be repaid if the person's situation recovers. This is why Jesus told his followers to make loans without expecting to be repaid.

> Give to the one who asks you, and do not turn away from
> the one who wants to borrow from you (Matt 5:42).

Jesus' principle of generosity was a restatement of a command in Deuteronomy.

> If there is a poor man among your brothers in any of the
> towns of the land that the Lord your God is giving you, do
> not be hard-hearted or tight-fisted toward your poor brother.
> Rather be open-handed and freely lend him whatever he

needs. Be careful not to harbour this wicked thought: "The seventh year, the year for cancelling debts, is near," so that you do not show ill will toward your needy brother and give him nothing. Give generously to him and do so without a grudging heart; then because of this the Lord your God will bless you in all your work and in everything you put your hand to. I command you to be open-handed toward the poor and needy in your land (Deut 15:7-11).

If someone gets into financial difficulty, another person in their neighbourhood who is better off should give them a loan to help them through the difficult time. No particular person is responsible for making the loan, but the neighbours of the person in trouble are expected to be generous.

Given that the loan might not be repaid, it would not be surprising if people were reluctant to make a loan to a person in trouble, but this is not acceptable to God. He expects people to be generous. He says that generosity to neighbours is a condition for receiving his economic blessing. This makes sense. A community in which everybody is contributing will be stronger than one in which many of the people are struggling with poverty.

Lenders have power over borrowers. This power can be used to intimidate the weaker person, but this divides the community and undermines its strength. The Torah requires a lender to treat a vulnerable person with respect.

When you make a loan of any kind to your neighbour, do not go into his house to get what he is offering as a pledge. Stay outside and let the man to whom you are making the loan bring the pledge out to you (Deut 24:10-11).

The person with power must not enter the poor person's house to create fear among their family or looking for valuables to claim.

In the modern world, poor people with no assets often have to go to loan sharks, who charge excessive interest rates, often up to fifty percent. If the poor person fails to pay the interest, it will be added to the loan, so in a very short time, the debt will become enormous. The lender often seizes all of the property of the poor person to cover the debt, and they are left destitute.

Efforts to help poor people must not harm them. Poor people must not be forced deeper into debt. If they cannot repay the loan, they are left no worse off than they were before they received it.

Loans and Interest

A person might need a loan to get their business started or to expand an existing one. If a loan is necessary, the term should be limited to seven years.

> At the end of every seven years you shall grant a release of debts. And this is the form of the release: Every creditor who has lent anything to his neighbour shall release it; he shall not require it of his neighbour or his brother (Deut 15:1).

The Instructions for Economic Life specify that interest cannot be charged to a brother, but it is legitimate for a loan to a stranger.

> You shall not charge interest to your brother, whether on money or food or anything else that may earn interest. To a stranger you may charge interest, but to your brother you shall not charge interest, that the Lord your God may bless you in everything you set your hand to in the land you are entering to possess (Deut 23:19-20).

Interest may be charged to a "stranger". The Hebrew word refers to a person who is not known. However, interest must not be charged on a loan to a "brother", because God's people must love their brothers and sisters and be generous in helping them. The scope of this instruction is narrower than the limit to seven years, which applies to both "brother" and "neighbour".

God's people should generally not need to borrow. Being in debt is the sign that God's blessing has been lost.

> There need be no poor people among you, for in the land the Lord our God... will richly bless you (Deut 15:4).

If God is blessing them, they should not need to borrow. However, some people will make mistakes and need to borrow to get ahead.

God's people must not borrow from the nations, but they may lend to them.

> For the Lord your God will bless you as he has promised, and you will lend to many nations but will borrow from none (Deut 15:6).

Borrowing from strangers is dangerous as it gives spiritual authority to people who do not honour God.

Security for Debt

A lender is entitled to security for their loan, but they must not take anything that is needed for the borrower's livelihood or safety.

> Do not take a pair of millstones—not even the upper one— as security for a debt, because that would be taking a man's livelihood as security (Deut 24:6).

Business equipment must not be taken as security because it would prevent the person from operating their business.

> If you take your neighbour's cloak as a pledge, return it to him by sunset, because his cloak is the only covering he has for his body. What else will he sleep in? When he cries out to me, I will hear, for I am compassionate (Ex 22:26-27; also Deut 24:12-13).

If personal effects are taken for security, they must be returned whenever they are needed. God will be blessed.

Land

Christians who dislike Leviticus miss out on one of the most important economic guidelines in the scriptures. God declared that he owned the land and it must not be sold permanently.

> The land must not be sold permanently, because the land is mine and you reside in my land as foreigners and strangers (Lev 25:23).

God owns the land. This command has massive implications. People can use the land, but they can never own it. The land must not be sold. All that can be sold is the crops that it will produce.

> You are to buy from your own people on the basis of the number of years since the jubilee. And they are to sell to you on the basis of the number of years left for harvesting crops. When the years are many, you are to increase the price, and when the years are few, you are to decrease the price, because what is really being sold to you is the number of crops (Lev 25:15-16).

Only the future crops can be sold. The land itself must not be sold because it belongs to God.

We must use land in a way that is pleasing to God. We must not do anything with the land that the owner would not do. If we damage the land, we are robbing God. The Instructions for Economic Life provided for the land to be rested during every seventh year (Lev 25:1-6). Those who take crops off the land must ensure that the land is regenerated and refreshed.

Losing the Land

Some people use their land productively and do well. Others misuse their land and get into financial difficulty. If a family gets into serious financial trouble, they might need to sell their land to settle their debts. However, the land must not be sold in perpetuity, because it belongs to God. All that can be sold is the crops produced between the present day and the next jubilee.

The Instructions for Economic Life protected families who become poor by allowing land that had been sold to be redeemed at the jubilee, which occurred every fifty years.

> You must provide for the redemption of the land (Lev 25:24).

If a debtor family has sold their land to a creditor to settle their debts, three things could happen.

1. A relative or neighbour should come to the aid of the debtor family and buy back the land from the creditor to whom it had been sold.

   > If one of your fellow Israelites becomes poor and sells some of their property, their nearest relative is to come and redeem what they have sold (Lev 25:25).

   The redeemer will pay the full price paid by the purchaser. This was a sacrifice as the redeemer of the land would receive very little. They might get some crops while they were getting the debtor family prepared to look after it again, but they will never own the land they have bought. This was essentially a gift from one person to another. The only benefit would be living in a strong community.

2. If no one redeems the land sold by a person in debt and they return to prosperity again, they can buy their family property back at any time.

   > If, however, there is no one to redeem it for them but later on they prosper and acquire sufficient means to redeem it themselves, they are to determine the value for the years since they sold it and refund the balance to the one to whom they sold it; they can then go back to their own property (Lev 25:26-27).

   The price will be set at the value of the crops that will be received between the sale day and the jubilee. They do not have to repay the full amount paid because the buyer has received crops from the land. The value of the land is the crops that it can produce.

3. If there is no redeemer and the person in trouble never recovers sufficiently to repurchase it, the buyer can only hold the land until the jubilee. The land must be returned to the family who sold it when the jubilee arrives.

> But if they do not acquire the means to repay, what was sold will remain in the possession of the buyer until the Year of Jubilee. It will be returned in the jubilee, and they can then go back to their property (Lev 25:28).

The buyer cannot buy the land permanently because it belongs to God. They only buy the harvests that will occur between the purchase date and the jubilee.

There are no penalties attached to the instruction for redeeming land because there is no government to enforce it. It was a voluntary instruction to ensure that wealth and productive assets did not get unevenly distributed. If one generation got into trouble and lost a productive asset, the next generation could get it back and make a fresh start.

The prophets spoke against those who accumulated land and houses.

> Woe to you who add house to house and join field to field till no space is left and you live alone in the land (Isaiah 5:8).

These people were breaching God's principle that land should be evenly distributed. They would not have been able to do this if they understood and applied the principle of the jubilee.

The concept of property described in the Instructions for Economic Life is not individualistic. Land was assigned to family groups. It is held in trust for the benefit of future generations of the family. Losing the land was a failure of trust that cursed later generations. God protected the family line be providing a way to remedy a mistake that could harm their future.

Extreme Poverty

If a person gets deep into debt, they might need to bond themselves to a prosperous person in return for them paying off all their debts

> If any of your people—Hebrew men or women—sell
> themselves to you and serve you six years, in the seventh
> year you must let them go free. And when you release them,
> do not send them away empty-handed.   Supply them
> liberally from your flock, your threshing floor and your
> winepress. Give to them as the Lord your God has blessed
> you. Remember that you were slaves in Egypt and the Lord
> your God redeemed you. That is why I give you this
> command today (Deut 15:12-15; cf Ex 21:2).

The prosperous person must settle all the debts of the destitute
person. In return for that, the poor person would agree to work
for them for up to seven years. As well as getting out of debt, they
would get the opportunity to learn from someone who has
managed life better. God's people must not give up their freedom
permanently, so the bond period must be limited to seven years,
even if that does not fully cover the outstanding debts.

When a bonded employee is set free, the person who has paid
the debts must be generous. They should send the person they
helped away with some working capital so they can get started
again.

> Do not consider it a hardship to set your servant free,
> because their service to you these six years has been worth
> twice as much as that of a hired hand. And the Lord your
> God will bless you in everything you do (Deut 15:18).

A person who is a perpetual miss-manager might decide they would
be better to remain as a bonded employee.

> But if your servant says to you, "I do not want to leave you,"
> because he loves you and your family and is well off with
> you, then take an awl and push it through his earlobe into
> the door, and he will become your servant for life. Do the
> same for your female servant (Deut 15:16-17).

Some people who are hopelessly incompetent may need someone
to manage for them. They could choose an employer who could
take care of them and their family and bond themselves to them.

This permanent bonded employment is voluntary. It is for the
benefit of the bonded employee, not for the person holding the
bond. The servant freely decides to be a servant. Since they

voluntarily became a servant for life, they are free to leave at any time.

Chattel slavery was not permitted by the Instructions for Economic Life. Kidnapping free people and forcing them into slavery was the same as murder (Ex 21:16; Deut 24:7). People who have been forced into slavery must be set free.

> If a slave has taken refuge with you, do not hand them over to their master. Let them live among you wherever they like and in whatever town they choose. Do not oppress them (Deut 23:15-16).

There should be no slaves among God's people. If a slave escaped from a different place and sought shelter in a community, they must not be returned to their owner. They are to be set free to live in the community. God's people are called to set people free, not to enslave and oppress them.

By the time of Jeremiah, the Instructions for Economic Life were being ignored in Judah. Jeremiah challenged the people because they had retained bonded servants beyond the seventh year (Jer 34:13-14). King Zedekiah and the leaders of the people decided to free all bonded servants because they were under threat from Babylon and they needed God's help (Jer 34:8-10). This was a wonderful event, but they quickly changed their minds and put those who were freed back into bondage again.

> But afterwards, they changed their minds and took back the servants they had freed and enslaved them again (Jer 34:11).

The word "enslaved" is a strong word (kabash). It means to "conquer, subjugate, or violate". These people had bonded themselves because they needed help to get out of debt. They had been set free (kophshim) but were now being enslaved by force, so their situation was made worse. Jeremiah prophesied,

> Therefore, this is what the Lord says: you have not proclaimed freedom to your own people. So I now proclaim 'freedom' for you —'freedom' to fall by the sword, plague and famine (Jer 34:17).

Jeremiah explained that failure to give people the freedom required by the Instructions for Economic Life would cause loss of freedom; in a nasty way, by the sword, plague and famine.

Security and Blessings

The Instructions for Economic Life provided economic security for everyone in society. Economic strength was based on love within a local community, not on a government or king. The motivations for acting on these instructions must be love: love of God and love of neighbour. The Instructions for Economic Life show how life can change if God's people love their neighbours.

3
Jesus' Economics

Life in Jesus' Time

The coming of the Roman Empire destroyed what was left of the community-based economy that God had provided for the children of Israel in his Instructions for Economic Life.

- The Sadducees and the priestly families who collaborated with the Romans were rewarded with large land holdings. The people who had previously owned them were turned into tenant farmers and had to hand over at least half of their crops as rent.

- The empire imposed exorbitant taxes on the ordinary people. This pushed most families into poverty. The tax collectors got rich and most of the people became poor (Luke 5:29).

- King Herod built an expensive temple in Jerusalem. His son built several new Roman cities. The governor of Judea built a new city of Caesarea Philippi. To pay for these building projects, the people had to pay heavy taxes.

- Debt and interest were used to impoverish people and to steal their land. When a borrower could not repay a loan, the lender would demand their land to settle the debt.

- For ordinary people, storing up wealth was impossible. If the Roman soldiers found coins or grain hidden in a house, they would often smash it.

- By Jesus' time, most families in Israel had no land. A few powerful families controlled most of the land. Tax collectors and soldiers would grab any surplus crops and most money that was earned. The people were left with very little to live on.
- Most people would have to find work each day as day-labourers to buy their food for that day. Jesus knew that the people who had followed him around the lake to listen to his teaching all day would be hungry. As they had not worked, they would have no food, and not be able to buy any.
- People were hungry all the time.
  During those days another large crowd gathered. Since they had nothing to eat, Jesus called his disciples to him and said, "I have compassion for these people; they have already been with me three days and have nothing to eat (Mark 8:1-3).
  Going without out food was common.

For the people of Israel, the Roman Empire was a terrible place to live. Land was concentrated in the hands of a wealthy few. Ordinary people struggled because most of what they produced would be taken by the Romans and the temple system. Life was brutal and extreme poverty was normal. People were looking for a messiah who would break the shackles of Rome and free them from the burden of debt and tax.

Change of Heart

When Jesus preached and taught in Galilee and Jerusalem, he responded to the situation the people were living in. When he challenged the people to repent, he was not criticising the people for their failure to produce the fruit of the Spirit. That was not possible because the Spirit had not yet been given.

Jesus called the people to repent of their failure to obey Moses and the prophets. Roman law and government had been imposed upon them, so they could not repent of failure to implement God's system of justice, but they could be challenged for their failure to implement the Instructions for Economic Life in their daily lives.

The households and families of Israel were divided from each other. They had stopped supporting each other, so the Roman soldiers and tax collectors could pick them off one at a time.

> If a kingdom is divided against itself, that kingdom cannot
> stand. If a house is divided against itself, that house cannot
> stand (Mark 3:24-25).

If the families of Galilee and Judea had stood together in solidarity and supported each other, they could have created a better life, despite the oppression of the Romans.

We interpret the Parable of the Sower as describing the response of people to the gospel. That makes sense after the cross and resurrection, but it did not make sense to Jesus' listeners. Jesus said, "the seed is the word of God" (Luke 8:11). For his listeners, the word of God was the Law and the Prophets, including the Instructions for Economic Life. This gift had been mostly wasted, as the devil had stolen it from their hearts. Many received the Instructions for Economic Life gladly, but fell away during a time of testing.

Many still accepted God's economic wisdom, but it was choked out by the "worries of life and the deceitfulness of riches" (Matt 13:22). Ordinary people were so beaten down by the "worries of life" that they did not think that it was practical to live by God's Instructions for Economic Life. The wealthy were sucked in by the "deceitfulness of riches" and did not want to disrupt their pleasure and comfort.

Despite Roman control, the people of Israel were still free to apply God's economic guidelines voluntarily, so they needed to repent of this failure and begin living their economic lives by his principles. The political situation was beyond their control, but they had significant control over their economic situation.

The Torah allowed a community of people to live together in peace, despite being ruled by a foreign power. God's Instructions for Economic Life do not need a king or political power, so faithful people can implement them within a hostile empire.

Jesus came to bring restoration to Israel. This would not be achieved through the Roman Empire, or by Jesus ruling in Jerusalem, but through the renewal of village and community life by the application of the Instructions for Economic Life.

Instructions for Economic Life

Jesus' teaching challenged his listeners to live according to God's Instructions for Economic Life. He had strong words for those who taught that the law was obsolete.

> Anyone who teaches... others to set aside one of the least of these commands will be called least in the kingdom of heaven, but whoever practices and teaches these commands will be called great in the kingdom of heaven. (Matt 5:19).

I do not know anyone who has tried to "become great in the kingdom" by teaching people how to "practice these commands". Yet that is what Jesus encouraged. His followers should be teaching people about the Instructions for Economic Life.

The Transfiguration confirmed the authority of the law and the prophets. After this event, Jesus gave an interesting response to a question about why Elijah must come first.

> Elijah has already come, and they did not recognise him, but have done to him everything they wished. Then the disciples understood that he was talking to them about John the Baptist (Matt 17:12-13).

Jesus explained that John the Baptist fulfilled the prophecy that Elijah would come. His role was not to create something new, but to restore all things. John could only restore something that had already existed. The key aspect of the Torah that he could restore in Galilee was the Instructions for Economic Life, as they were relevant to the daily lives of the people. This is why John preached about economic issues. When the people asked him what they should do, he told them to change their economic behaviour (Luke 3:10-14). Jesus validated John's message after the transfiguration.

Jesus condemned the Teachers of the Law and the Pharisees. They had twisted the law into a burden by providing the people with excuses for ignoring the Instructions for Economic Life.

> Woe to you Pharisees, because you give God a tenth of your mint, rue and all other kinds of garden herbs, but you neglect *justice* and the *love* of God. You should have practised the latter without leaving the former undone (Luke 11:42).

> And you experts in the law, woe to you, because you load people down with burdens they can hardly carry, and you yourselves will not lift one finger to help them (Luke 11:46).

When Jesus taught about economic issues, he always pointed back to the Instructions for Economic Life. He sometimes adapted them to be applicable in a culture ruled by a foreign power, but he did not change the underlying principles because they are rooted in love of God and love of neighbour (Lev 19:18). Jesus always affirmed the Instructions for Economic Life.

Love One Another

Jesus agreed that loving God was the greatest commandment.

> The most important one is this: 'Hear, O Israel: The Lord our God, the Lord is one. Love the Lord your God with all your heart and with all your soul and with all your mind and with all your strength.' The second is this: 'Love your neighbour as yourself'. There is no commandment greater than these (Mark 12:29-31).

Love of neighbour was the second greatest commandment. It was the heart of the Torah teaching and energised the Instructions for Economic Life. Jesus gave a new commandment.

> A new command I give you: Love one another. As I have loved you, so you must love one another (John 13:34).

Giving a new commandment was a little strange, as Jesus had already affirmed the two greatest commandments. However, he was not really giving a new commandment but shifting the old one into a new environment. The Torah commanded people to love their neighbour. This made sense in a tribal culture in an agricultural economy, where a neighbour would usually be a relative or a member of the same tribal group.

In New Testament times, the world had changed, and it was impossible to go back to the tribal culture of Moses' time. Jesus acknowledged this in the parable of the Good Samaritan when he extended the definition of a neighbour to include any person encountered during daily life. This updated the command to a world where people lived apart from their tribal and family groups.

Jesus refocused the command to "love your neighbour" into "love one another". Love continued, but the object of love changed. This kept the commandment relevant because "love one another" can be applied anywhere, including cities and industrial societies. Jesus shifted the fulfilment of the law from families and tribes to families and communities brought together by the gospel.

We think about "loving one another" in an abstract way. It would have been different for Jesus' listeners. They understood what loving one another meant, because it was no different from loving your neighbour, and they knew what that meant. Loving your neighbour encompassed all the Instructions for Economic Life contained in the law. Loving one another would be the same.

Changing the object from "neighbour" to "one another" shifted the application of the Instructions for Economic Life and the judicial laws of crime and punishment from the tribal groups of Israel to groups of people choosing to follow Jesus.

When Jesus told us to love one another, he extended our social and economic responsibility to everyone in our neighbourhood. They should be treated as neighbours according to the Instructions for Economic Life. The church of Jerusalem recorded in Acts was an attempt to restore God's social model in a city by applying the Instructions for Economic Life.

Sharing

John the Baptist challenged people to share their food and clothing with those in need.

> Anyone who has two shirts should share with the one who has none, and anyone who has food should do the same (Luke 3:11).

He challenged the soldiers to stop extorting taxes that they were not entitled to take. This was common practice at the time.

> Don't extort money and don't accuse people falsely—be content with your pay (Luke 3:14).

John pushed people back to the Instructions for Economic Life.

Jesus also challenged the people to implement the Instructions for Economic Life by giving generously to those in need.

> Give to everyone who asks you, and if anyone takes what belongs to you, do not demand it back (Luke 6:30).

This is loving your neighbour. It should not be done out of obligation, but must be motivated by the love of God.

> Be merciful, just as your Father is merciful (Luke 6:36).

Those who love God will be merciful like him.

Debt

Many of the people living in Galilee and Judea were in debt. Their debts were often owed to their countrymen. Jesus' parable suggested a solution.

> Two people owed money to a certain moneylender. One owed him five hundred denarii, and the other fifty. Neither of them had the money to pay him back, so he forgave the debts of both (Luke 7:41-42)?

Cancelling debts was not a revolutionary idea, but what the Torah required. All debts were to be cancelled after seven years.

Cancellation of debt was the theme of another parable (Matt 18:21-31). A man who had been forgiven a huge debt refused to forgive someone who owed him a small amount that he owed and had him thrown in prison.

> The master called the servant in. 'You wicked servant,' he said, 'I cancelled all that debt of yours because you begged me to. Shouldn't you have had mercy on your fellow servant just as I had on you?' In anger his master handed him over to the jailers (Matt 18:32-34)

In many ways, the sin of the first servant was worse. The money he owed was a business loan. The loan he made to the other servant was a loan to someone in poverty. The Torah required this loan to be interest-free, and it should have been cancelled after seven years if the debtor could not repay it.

Jesus told people that they should not go to the Roman courts to recover debts.

> Settle matters quickly with your adversary who is taking you to court. Do it while you are still together on the way, or your adversary may hand you over to the judge, and the judge may hand you over to the officer, and you may be thrown into prison. Truly I tell you, you will not get out until you have paid the last penny (Matt 5:25-26).

Creditors were regular users of the courts in Judea. If they followed God's standards and cancelled the debts, they would not need to run the risk of going to an unreliable court. It would be far more sensible to cancel debts after seven years as the Torah required. (The issue of debt is covered in more detail in chapter 8).

The Lord's prayer contained a commitment to cancelling debts.

> And forgive us our debts,
> as we also have forgiven our debtors (Matt 6:12).

Jesus just assumes that creditors will cancel the debts of their debtors. If his listeners did this, huge blessings would flow.

Caring for the Poor

Jesus challenged his followers to feed people who are hungry.

> For I was hungry and you gave me something to eat, I was thirsty and you gave me something to drink, I was a stranger and you invited me in, I needed clothes and you clothed me, I was sick and you looked after me, I was in prison and you came to visit me (Matt 25:35-36).

Followers of Jesus are expected to share food with their neighbours. Giving to the poor made economic sense, because storing up wealth would attract tax collectors and thieves.

> Do not store up for yourselves treasures on earth, where moths and vermin destroy, and where thieves break in and steal. But store up for yourselves treasures in heaven, where moths and vermin do not destroy, and where thieves do not break in and steal (Matt 6:19-20)

Storing up treasure was impossible in Galilee and Judea. If the moths and vermin did not destroy it, the soldiers and tax collectors would. Moths and vermin were probably a cheeky reference to the Romans and their tax collectors. Giving to the poor would gain "reward from your Father in heaven" (Matt 6:1). This treasure cannot be stolen.

Interest-Free Loans

Jesus challenged people to lend to those in need without expecting anything in return.

> Give to the one who asks you, and do not turn away from the one who wants to borrow from you (Matt 5:42).

This was an application of the Instructions for Economic Life.

> If you lend to those from whom you expect repayment, what credit is that to you? Even sinners lend to sinners, expecting to be repaid in full. But love your enemies, do good to them, and lend to them without expecting to get anything back (Luke 6:34-35).

Jesus' words encouraged interest-free loans to the poor.

Most people will lend if they know they will be repaid, and especially if they can earn interest. Jesus expected his followers to be different. They must lend to the poor expecting nothing in return. This was not a new idea. It was the Torah principle of interest-free loans to the poor.

Employers

Permanent employment was rare in Jesus' time, so large numbers of landless people faced a hand-to-mouth existence doing casual work whenever they could get it. The shrewd steward in Jesus' parable understood the benefit of permanent employment.

> My master is taking away my job. I'm not strong enough to
> dig, and I'm ashamed to beg (Luke 16:3).

If he lost his job as a steward, his choices were sparse. He was not lazy or proud, but very realistic. He was not strong enough for the physical work of a day labourer, so he would have to beg, and that would be hard.

In the parable of the Vineyard Workers, Jesus told employers that they should be considerate (Matt 20:1-16). The employer promised to pay the employees who only worked for part of a day "what is right" (v 4). The Greek word is "dikaion", which means righteous. This employer wanted to do the right thing, but what is right is specified in the Instructions for Economic Life.

The employer offered the workers who worked for the entire day a denarius. They accepted because this was the typical pay for a day's work. The people who had only worked for a few hours were paid the same as those who had worked for a whole day. This was a correct application of Deuteronomy 24:15. The employer knew that the people who had only worked for an hour would not be able to earn any more money until the next day.

They were on the poverty line, living from hand to mouth. Having become their neighbour by employing them, the vineyard owner had an obligation to pay them enough to provide their families with food until they could work again on the next day. At that time, a person needed a denarius to buy a day's food for their family. The employer was considerate. He paid each person a wage sufficient for them to live until the next day when they would have the opportunity to earn some more. When challenged, the employer explained his actions.

> Don't I have the right to do what I want with my own money? Or are you envious because I am generous (Matt 20:15).

Being considerate and providing for a neighbour is more important than treating everyone the same.

Land

Jesus challenged those who had accumulated land to give it away. When a man inquired about eternal life, he claimed to have kept all the commandments since he was a boy.

> Jesus looked at him and loved him. "One thing you lack," he said. "Go, sell everything you have and give to the poor, and you will have treasure in heaven. Then come, follow me." At this the man's face fell. He went away sad, because he had great wealth (Mark 10:21-22).

In those days, most wealth was land and the only way to accumulate land and hold it was to collaborate with the Romans. This man claimed to have kept the commandments since he was a boy (Matt 8:20), but Jesus explained that he was wrong. He had honoured the Ten Commandments, but he had ignored the Instructions for Economic Life. His land was "unrighteous wealth" To be righteous, he needed to sell his land and give it away (more on land in chapter 9).

Part 2

Application for Followers of Jesus

Part Two applies God's Instructions for Economic Life to modern society. God does not expect the people of the world to live according to these instructions. They have been deceived by the spiritual powers of evil into desiring things of the world and pursuing wealth and prosperity (1 John 2:15-17). However, he expects people who have chosen to serve Jesus to apply his wisdom in their lives and communities.

These instructions are only practical amongst people who are being the church where they live. They can apply God's instructions without the need for government enforcement while continuing to live in a world that is dominated by the existing power systems. They do not need to wait for the existing system to collapse. Instead, they can prepare for that season by establishing Kingdom Communities where God's will is done. God's economy will become a witness and sign to the world that has lost its way.

The advance of the gospel should turn the economic world upside down. Jesus gave a stark message about wealth and poverty:

> Looking at his disciples, he said:
> Blessed are you who are poor,
> for yours is the kingdom of God.
> Blessed are you who hunger now,
> for you will be satisfied (Luke 6:20-21).

These are strong words. Jesus promised an economic revolution. The poor will be blessed and the rich will experience woes. The hungry will be satisfied, but those who have plenty already will be disappointed. This is the reverse of the way things happen in the world, so what did Jesus mean?

The radical change that Jesus was promising cannot come about through government programs. The economic world will be turned upside down as followers of Jesus obey his teaching and apply the Instructions for Economic Life:

- Getting rid of unrighteous wealth
- Giving and sharing
- Generous buying and selling
- Sharing land
- Cancelling debts
- Transforming business activities

These themes are covered in the next few chapters.

4

Unrighteous Wealth

Jesus' teaching about unrighteous wealth shocked his listeners. He insisted that unrighteous wealth must be given away. Even his twelve disciples found this hard to accept. His modern followers get round his blunt message by saying that money is neutral and that what we do with it is what is important. They say that it acceptable to have heaps of money provided it is used wisely. This is not true. The character of wealth is determined by the way it was obtained. Unrighteous wealth can never be fine.

When Jesus defined unrighteous wealth, he was re-emphasising the standards of the Instructions for Economic Life given to Moses. He taught specifically about unrighteous wealth in the parable of the Shrewd Manager (Luke 16:1-13). This parable is hard to interpret, so it is mostly ignored. The translations do not help much, because they dull the meaning of the parable by talking about worldly wealth. However, the parable has a very precise message.

Background
In Jesus time, the land had been accumulated into large estates. This land had often been confiscated from innocent and ordinary people. The Romans handed out land to the people who were loyal to them. Herod did the same. In this environment, the easiest way to get rich was through collusion with political power.

Many of the people who lost their land were forced to become tenant farmers. In return for the use of the land, they would have to give the landowner a big chunk of their crops. The landlords held all the power, so they could get a good return, with very little risk. A troublesome tenant farmer could easily be replaced with another because the countryside was full of landless peasants, so these deals were stacked in the property owner's favour.

Tenant farming was a miserable life. The tenant did all the work and carried all of the risks, but got very little in return. If the crops were good, the landlord would get most of it. If the weather was bad and the crops failed, the landowner would still take their due, and the tenant farmer would be left to starve. In a really bad year, the entire crop might not be enough to meet the claim of the property owner. The landlord would take the crop, and add the shortfall to the payment due from next year's crop. Tenant farmers were usually poor.

The only risk for landowners was falling out of favour with the political powers and having their land confiscated. This is why the Sadducees and the Herodians were so afraid of upsetting the Romans. They were big landowners with a lot to lose.

Jesus' listeners knew that accumulating land by political collusion was contrary to the Instructions for Economic Life. Joshua had distributed the land equally among the people. Every family in Israel was given a share of the land. If a family fell into debt, there was a process for restoring their land back to their children (Lev 25). Accumulating land was strictly prohibited.

The Parable

The shrewd manager was asked to give an account of his management. He was accused of not earning enough money for his landlord, probably by someone who wanted his job.

The rich man owned land and gained his income by renting it to tenant farmers in return for a share of their crops. His manager was responsible for organising agreements with the tenant farmers and recording their debts. The bills referred to in the parable had been written by the shrewd manager. One tenant had to pay a 100 cors of wheat each year for his use of the land. Another with an olive grove had to hand over 100 batos of oil.

The rich man had gained control of his land by co-operating with the Roman invaders. His manager knew that the rich man's income was unrighteous wealth, but he had used his power to squeeze as much as possible out of the tenants. He had signed the original agreements, so he knew the amounts were excessive.

The rich man treated the shrewd manager badly. He had done many deals that favoured the landlord, but when he heard rumours, the rich man acted on them without giving the shrewd manager a chance to explain. He terminated the manager's position and demanded a full record of his accounts.

The shrewd manager had the power to change the agreements. When the rich man demanded his records back, his objective changed. Before returning the record of outstanding debts, he reduced the amounts owed to make friends with people whose lives he had made miserable by imposing exorbitant rents.

The shrewd manager allowed the tenants to change their debts to a more reasonable amount. The rents were unfair when they were agreed, so he believed he was justified in making arbitrary changes to the amounts owed. By reducing the payment to 80 cors of wheat, the shrewd manager made the tenant's wheat farming economic. By halving the payment of olive oil to 50 batos, the manager made the olive grove economic again.

When the shrewd manager changed the bills, the rich man praised his behaviour. He had gained his wealth dishonestly, so he respected the unscrupulous behaviour of his manager. One crook recognised another. The key to the parable in Luke 16:9.

> I tell you, use **unrighteous wealth** to gain friends for yourselves, so that when it is gone, you will be welcomed into eternal dwellings.

Jesus said that his followers should use their unrighteous wealth or "wealth of injustice" to make friends for the Kingdom. The only way to do this is to give it away.

The main message of the parable is the distinction between "righteous wealth" and "unrighteous wealth".

> So if you have not been faithful with **unrighteous wealth**, who will trust you with true riches (Luke 16:11)?

This parable is the first of a series told by Jesus that builds on this distinction. Jesus' message is blunt. People holding unrighteous wealth will not be trusted with spiritual blessing.

Righteous Wealth

If a person works hard and saves some of their earnings, their savings are righteous wealth. If they use their saving to buy assets that make them productive, those assets are righteous wealth.

If a person starts a business selling goods and services that people need for a price agreed without coercion or deception, the retained earnings of the business are righteous wealth. Righteous wealth is gained through hard work, honest trade and diligent investment. We can use righteous wealth to advance the Kingdom, but it has limited value. True riches are found in Jesus.

Unrighteous Wealth

Unrighteous wealth is "mammona adikia". It could also be translated as "wealth of injustice". It refers to wealth obtained through activities contrary to God's will, particularly those that are unjust. Jesus did not define unrighteous wealth because his listeners knew what he meant. Jesus was referring to wealth gained contrary to the Instructions for Economic Life.

In Hebrew writing, an idea is often repeated in a slightly different form, but with the same meaning. Jesus used this method to explain unrighteous wealth.

> If you have not been faithful with unrighteous wealth, who will trust you with true riches?
> And if you have not been faithful with another man's wealth, who will give you what is your own (Luke 16:11-12)?

The message of these two verses is the same. In verse 11, Jesus referred to "unrighteous wealth". In verse 12, he described it as "another man's wealth". He was explaining that "unrighteous wealth" really belongs to another person. The person with unrighteous wealth has taken wealth that belongs to someone else. Income or wealth that had been gained by practices that are forbidden in the Instructions for Economic Life is unrighteous because it really belongs to someone else.

Categories of Unrighteous Wealth

The following are the main categories of unrighteous wealth.

- Stolen goods and possessions become unrighteous wealth.
- Income gained by deception is unrighteous wealth.
- Income earned by producing and selling products that are harmful to the people consuming them is unrighteous wealth.
- Excessive profits gained by hoarding food during a crisis is unrighteous wealth (Prov 11:26; James 5:1-5).
- Wages held back from the poor are unrighteous wealth.
- Interest earned from lending to people who cannot afford it is unrighteous wealth.
- Income gained through unjust debt is unrighteous wealth (this is discussed more fully in chapter 8).
- Lending to people who cannot afford repayment and seizing the assets that have been pledged as security when they default is unrighteous wealth.
- Many large land-holdings are unrighteous wealth. God hates the accumulation of large areas of land and wants it evenly distributed. He created the earth for all humans and wants everyone to have some land, so they can feed themselves.
- The riches of most royal families are unrighteous wealth.
- The accumulation of houses is often unrighteous wealth. The prophets spoke against those who accumulated land and houses (Is 5:8).
- In the modern world, residential housing is a popular investment, but this can be unrighteous wealth. Excess demand pushes up the price of dwellings, which produces good capital gains, but the benefit to the investor makes someone else worse off. For example, a young person trying to buy a house finds their savings don't go as far.

  Investment in housing is unproductive. It does not increase the productivity of the economy. House price inflation transfers wealth from savers to property speculators. If people with more than one house were to sell them, house prices would fall and young people would find them easier to afford.

- Counterfeiters used to replace some of the gold or silver in coins with cheaper metals and keep the extra gold. Kings usually corrupted their currency in the same way. Modern banks do a similar thing by inflating their country's currency. Wealth obtained by debasing the currency is unrighteous wealth, whether it is done by a counterfeiter or a government.

  > See how the faithful city
  > has become a prostitute!
  > She once was full of justice;
  > righteousness used to dwell in her—
  > but now… your silver has become dross (Is 1:21-22).

  Those who become wealthy through debasing or inflating the currency are creating unrighteous wealth for themselves.

- In the modern world, people have found less direct ways to take advantage of the debasement or inflation of the currency. Many people have become wealthy by investing in real estate to capture the capital gains that come through inflation of property prices. These gains are often amplified by using borrowed money to pay for the properties.

  Large returns are earned through an activity that produces no benefit for the economy. The high returns are dependent on continued price inflation caused by the government manipulating the currency. Collecting capital gains generated by inflation is sharing in the deceitful activities of currency counterfeiters. Wealth obtained from capital gains from highly leveraged investments in real estate is usually unrighteous wealth. The prophets condemned this practice.

  > Woe to him who builds his house by unjust gain (Hab 2:9).

  Purchasing land or buildings with highly-leveraged debt and relying on inflation to wipe it out produces unrighteous wealth.

- Government-created inflation rewards debtors at the expense of people on fixed income. This is often invisible theft. Those who benefit are "receivers" of stolen wealth.

- Land that has been acquired contrary to the Instructions for Economic Life is unrighteous wealth (see chapter 9).

- The wealth of most political families is unrighteous wealth.

- Property and profit received through collusion with political powers is unrighteous wealth. People with political power often protect their positions by providing land and property to their supporters. The people who were rich in Jesus' time gained their wealth by participating in the Roman political system. Theirs was unrighteous wealth.
- In the modern world, governments often give a group of people monopoly power over an aspect of the economy, eg import licenses, mining licenses, railway concessions. These monopoly powers and licenses enable them to become very wealthy, but this is unrighteous wealth. Many wealthy families first gained their wealth in this way.
- Limited liability laws allow a business to take excessive risks and then leave their creditors (often small contractors) carrying the burden when they default. Wealth gained through limited liability laws could be unrighteous wealth.
- Activities motivated by greed produce unrighteous wealth
- The excessive celebrity and executive salaries proliferating in the modern world are often unrighteous wealth.
- If the Holy Spirit is prompting someone to assist a neighbour in financial difficulty by giving them an interest-free loan and they refuse, the money not lent becomes unrighteous wealth.
- If the Holy Spirit is prompting someone to assist a neighbour in financial difficulty by redeeming their property and they refuse to assist, their money becomes unrighteous wealth.

Business activity that relies on activities contrary to the Instructions for Economic Life usually produces unrighteous wealth. Much modern wealth is unrighteous wealth.

Christians and Unrighteous Wealth

The shrewd manager understood the difference between unrighteous wealth and righteous wealth. Christians need to understand the difference too because many hold unrighteous wealth that is blighting their lives.

- Some Christians have unrighteous wealth that they accumulated before they came to faith.

- Some Christians have inherited unrighteous wealth. The process of inheritance does not make it righteous.
- Many Christians are engaged in activities that produce unrighteous wealth.

Transforming Unrighteous Wealth

There are only two ways to transform unrighteous wealth.
- Giving it away (preferably to those from whom it was taken, but that is not always possible).
- God's judgment (which is compulsory giving).

1. Give Away

Jesus said that unrighteous wealth should be given away.

> Sell your possessions and give to the poor. Provide purses for yourselves that will not wear out, a treasure in heaven that will never fail, where no thief comes near and no moth destroys (Luke 12:33).

Because unrighteous wealth was so prevalent at that time, Jesus frequently told his hearers to give away their possessions.

If it is known who the unrighteous wealth was stolen from, restitution should be fourfold as required by Exodus 22:1. If it was general fraud, the response should be very generous giving, particularly to the class of people who have suffered.

Zacchaeus is an example of a new believer giving away his unrighteous wealth. He did not need to ask Jesus what to do. Being a good Jew, he was familiar with the Instructions for Economic Life. When he realised that Jesus loved him, he spontaneously put them into practice. He made fourfold restitution for what he had stolen and gave generously from money obtained by deceit.

The giving away of unrighteous wealth should not be indiscriminate as that would be pointless. The wealth should be given to neighbours and "one anothers", who need help to get back on their feet. The giving should be designed to help struggling people get to a place where they can manage for themselves.

When a person becomes a follower of Jesus, the Holy Spirit will convict them about the unrighteous wealth that they own. They should be encouraged to give it away.

The ministry of the deacon was established to facilitate this giving. Deacons are people who were skilled in managing their households and their work. They channel much of the giving because they can teach others how to manage their households better to stay out of debt. (The ministry of the Deacon is described more fully in my book called Being Church Where We Live).

Much of the wealth held in the western world is unrighteous wealth. This wealth is a consequence of gospel failure. When the gospel is truly effective, large amounts of unrighteous wealth will be given away. What happened in the early church should be normal. If the gospel advances in the western world over the next few decades, we should see huge amounts of unrighteous wealth being given away. This amazing event will transform the world.

2. Judgment

The other remedy for unrighteous wealth is judgment. God has promised that those who accumulate unrighteous wealth will be ruined. The Psalmist was envious of the prosperity of the wicked.

> I envied the arrogant when I saw the prosperity of the wicked.
> They have no struggles; their bodies are healthy and strong.
> They are free from common human burdens (Ps 73:3-5).

God gave him a glimpse of their future.

> Surely you place them on slippery ground; you cast them
> down to ruin. How suddenly are they destroyed, completely
> swept away by terrors (Ps 73:18-19).

They will be cast down to ruin.

> The wicked borrow and do not repay, but the righteous give
> generously; those the Lord blesses will inherit the land, but
> those he curses will be destroyed (Psalm 37:21-22).

The wicked will eventually lose their wealth.

> The house of the righteous contains great treasure,
> but the income of the wicked brings ruin (Prov 15:6).
>
> Dishonest money dwindles away (Prov 13:11)

James gave a similar warning.

> Now listen, you rich people, weep and wail because of the
> misery that is coming on you (James 5:1)

Those who hold unrighteous wealth will often prosper for a few generations, but their downfall inevitably comes. Prophets will challenge the selfishness of people who cling to their unrighteous wealth, because the judgment they cause will harm everyone in their society, not just the rich.

Responsibilities

Jesus did not give governments responsibility for confiscating unrighteous wealth. Confiscated wealth remains unrighteous wealth. Unrighteous wealth that a government transfers to another person continues to be unrighteous wealth. The only way to escape the clutches of unrighteous wealth is to give it away.

- When the state confiscates unrighteous wealth, it remains unrighteous wealth.
- Unrighteous wealth that is given away becomes righteous wealth.

When people in the book of Acts sold their property and gave it away, they were mostly getting rid of unrighteous wealth. The fact that Ananias and Saphira had problems giving suggests that it was unrighteous wealth.

Switching Allegiance

The shrewd manager shifted his allegiance from the rich man to the people who owed him money. This represents the shift in loyalty we make when deciding to follow Jesus. The shrewd manager knew that a person shifting allegiance must make a clean break.

> No one can serve two masters. Either you will hate the one and love the other, or you will be devoted to the one and despise the other (Luke 16:13).

Many new Christians fail to do this. They hang onto that unrighteous wealth that was important in their old life, but this divided loyalty is dangerous.

The shrewd manager had chosen to serve a dishonest man. He knew that most of the wealth of the rich man was "unrighteous wealth", but he chose to serve him anyway. He gave his allegiance to the wrong person. It seemed to be in a good role, but when he least expected it, the rich man turned against him for no reason. That often happens to those who give allegiance to evil.

Once the shrewd manager was caught out, he switched allegiance to his clients. Having made that choice, he did what was good for them, hoping that they would look after him. He adjusted the debts, so that,

> people will welcome me into their homes (Luke 16:4).

Dealing with unrighteous wealth is easier for a person who belongs to a strong community. Living close to other believers who share what they have brings greater blessing than unrighteous wealth.

People who trust in unrighteous wealth cannot be trusted with true riches.

> Whoever can be trusted with very little can also be trusted with much, and whoever is dishonest with very little will also be dishonest with much. So if you have not been trustworthy in handling unrighteous wealth, who will trust you with true riches (Luke 16:10-11)?

People clinging to unrighteous wealth will not be trusted with the treasure of the Spirit. We cannot convert unrighteous wealth by using it for God while keeping it for ourselves.

Discerning Unrighteous Wealth

There are no simple rules for distinguishing between righteous and unrighteous wealth. Some will be obvious. The shrewd manager had worked for the rich man, so he knew that his wealth was earned in unrighteous ways. People who have served sin should be able to recognise the fruits of sin.

The Holy Spirit will convict those who seek him earnestly if their wealth is unrighteous. We can trust him to do this if we listen honestly. Christians make various rationalisations to justify their unrighteous wealth, but the Holy Spirit is not fooled.

Unrighteous wealth can usually be discerned by examining the way it was acquired. It will often have been obtained through deception, theft, manipulation or dishonesty. In Jesus' time, it was often acquired through collusion with the political and religious powers. The problem is the same now, but the form will be different. Governments often give a group of people economic benefits that enable them to become wealthy.

Unrighteous wealth is not an objective standard that can be decided by a judge. Nor can it be decided by other Christians or elders. Only the person who holds the wealth knows how it was obtained, so they must decide whether it is unrighteous wealth or not. An elder can explain the concept, but a new believer must assess their own wealth and determine its status. Only the property owner can decide how much of their wealth is unrighteous.

Zacchaeus decided that half of his wealth was unrighteous wealth and gave it away. Likewise, the property owner must decide themselves what they will do with their unrighteous wealth. They can ask Christian elders or deacons for advice, but their decisions must be a personal choice, not compulsion.

Elders must not force new Christians to give away their wealth, whether it is unrighteous or not. The Ananias and Saphira incident probably occurred because people were coming under inappropriate pressure to give away wealth (Acts 5:1-10). Jesus' teaching is not the basis for compulsory income redistribution, either by the church or political power.

Barnabas

Barnabas brought his money to the disciples when he realised it was unrighteous wealth.

> Joseph, a Levite from Cyprus, whom the apostles called
> Barnabas (which means Son of Encouragement), sold a field
> he owned and brought the money and put it at the apostles'
> feet (Acts 4:36-37).

Barnabas was a Levite, so he was not entitled to own land in Israel (Num 26:62). When he came to faith in Jesus, the illegal ownership of land would have weighed on his conscience. He probably could not return the land to its rightful owner (Lev 25:13), so he sold the land and gave the money to support people in need.

The word used for possessions in Acts 2:45, 4:34 and Acts 5:1 is "ktema" or "ktetor" This is not the word generally used for possessions in the New Testament (uparxis). These nouns are derived from the verb "ktaomai". It means "acquire" or "gain control over". It refers to property that was acquired, not bought.

"Ktema" refers to unrighteous wealth that has been acquired by wickedness or "acquired as a reward for wickedness". The property sold by Christians like Barnabas and Ananias had been acquired through unrighteous activities.

Lazarus and the Rich Man

Jesus continued to teach about the dangers of unrighteous wealth in the parable of the Rich Man and Lazarus (Luke 16:19-31). Most Christians see this as teaching about heaven and hell, but this misses the point of the parable. It follows on from the parable of the Shrewd manager, in which Jesus articulated the concept of unrighteous wealth. The parable of the Rich Man and Lazarus continues this theme. Jesus was warning that the soul of the person who owns unrighteous wealth is in serious danger.

The rich man took his riches as a sign he had inherited the blessing of Abraham. He ignored Lazarus, assuming that because he was poor, he must be cursed.

Like many poor people, Lazarus would have enjoyed a few scraps of food from the rich man's rubbish bin, but he was shut out from that too. The only trickle down from this table was the dogs licking his sores, but that was small comfort.

When the two men died, the rich man discovered his assessment was wrong. Although he had gained much wealth, he did not have God's blessing. Now he was in agony. Why did he end up on the wrong side of the great divide? Jesus' listeners would have understood. He wore a purple robe, symbolising royalty, privilege and power. Purple indicates a government role linked to the Roman Empire, so his wealth was unrighteous wealth.

The rich man asked Abraham to send someone to his brothers to warn them. Abraham said that the Law and the Prophets should be enough. The Instructions for Economic Life given to Moses already explained unrighteous wealth very clearly. The prophets confirmed the seriousness of unrighteous wealth. The rich man's brothers already had everything that they needed to know.

The rich man had ignored the Instructions for Economic Life and got on with becoming rich. He thought that he was inheriting the promise of Abraham, but he was actually ignoring God's standard for righteous wealth. This left him on the wrong side of the eternal divide. Lazarus had experienced the bad things condemned by the law, so he arrived at a place of blessing. He was the true son of Abraham.

The Pharisee and the Tax Collector

We think this is a parable about hypocrisy, but this is not quite right (Luke 18:9-14). The parable has a strong economic message. Hypocrisy is pretending that you are better than you are. The Pharisee was not pretending. He was wrong about righteousness.

This parable is part of a series of parables about unrighteous wealth. Jesus directed it towards people who "trusted in themselves that they are righteous". The Pharisee assumed his wealth was righteous because he tithed a tenth of "everything that he acquired". Jesus said that he did not go home justified before God.

Tithing on unrighteous wealth does not make it righteous. The righteousness of wealth depends on how it is acquired, not on how much is tithed. Acquisition of wealth must be consistent with God's Instructions for Economic Life. The Pharisee failed to meet that standard, so he was benefiting from unrighteous wealth. His wealth looked fine on the outside, but it was actually no better than the tax collector's.

The tax collector was not an innocent bureaucrat. Tax collectors were instruments of the Roman Empire. They extracted as much wealth from the people as they could get. They paid what they owed to the Romans, and kept the rest for themselves. Being a tax collector was a good way to becomes rich, but it was unrighteous wealth.

The tax collector in the parable knew that his wealth was unrighteous, so asked God for mercy. The Pharisee believed his wealth was righteous, so he did not realise that he needed mercy. Both men in the parable were owners of unrighteous wealth. The tax collector knew it, whereas the Pharisee did not.

The message of the parable is that the person who acquires unrighteous wealth is no better than the tax collector. They might do good things with their wealth, but that does not change its character. Tithing of unrighteous wealth does not make it right.

The Rich Ruler

Jesus did not just tell parables about the dangers of unrighteous wealth; he applied his teaching to real-life situations.

Unrighteous Wealth

When a rich man inquired how to inherit eternal life, Jesus asked him about the commandments. The man insisted that he had kept them all, including the command not to steal. I presume he mentioned this one because he had heard Jesus' views about wealth.

Jesus bluntly told him to sell everything he owned and give it to the poor. The reason that he had to get rid of everything was that it was unrighteous wealth. The only way to make it right and comply with the standard of the law was to give it away.

The rich man said he had kept the commandments since he was a boy (Luke 18:21), but he was wrong. He had kept the Ten Commandments, but ignored the Instructions for Economic Life.

Luke records that the man became sad, because "he was very wealthy". This man was a ruler. In Jesus' time, a ruler was an agent of the Roman empire. Running the country on behalf of the Romans was a great way to become rich without having to engage in robbery. To retain this position, he would have colluded with the Roman political and military system.

Wealth gained by collusion with political power is unrighteous wealth. It is tainted with evil, so it cannot come into the Kingdom.

> You still lack one thing. Sell everything you have and give to
> the poor, and you will have treasure in heaven (Luke 18:22).

This stark warning made the man very sad because he had great wealth. Jesus drew a tough conclusion.

> How hard it is for the rich to enter the kingdom of God!
> Indeed, it is easier for a camel to go through the eye of a
> needle than for someone who is rich to enter the kingdom
> of God (Luke 18:24-25)

Some of Jesus' listeners thought he was saying it was impossible for rich people to be saved, but they were wrong. He was explaining that it very hard for an owner of unrighteous wealth because it gets a hold that is hard to break.

Jesus was explaining that a rich man could enter heaven, but it must be done God's way. A rich man could only get rid of his unrighteous wealth by giving it away to the poor. Unrighteous wealth cannot come into the Kingdom. Those who cannot leave it behind must stay out.

Zacchaeus

Zacchaeus is an example of new believer giving away his unrighteous wealth. When Jesus came to dine with him, he stood up and said,

> Look, Lord! Here and now I give half of my possessions to the poor, and if I have cheated anybody out of anything, I will pay back four times the amount (Luke 19:8).

This was not a grand gesture to impress Jesus. He knew that he was the owner of unrighteous wealth. Tax collectors became rich by stealing from their fellow citizens with standover tactics. Zacchaeus was entitled to a fee for his services, but most of his wealth was unrighteous wealth.

He wanted to enter the Kingdom of God, so he knew that he had to get rid of his unrighteous wealth. He offered to give fourfold restitution to anyone he had stolen from, as required by the Instructions for Economic Life (Ex 22:1). He no longer knew who most of his wealth was stolen from, so he could not make restitution for it. He dealt with this by giving half of his possessions to the poor. Zacchaeus knew that he could not take his unrighteous wealth into the Kingdom, so he got rid of it.

Temptation

Many people who come to Jesus will have unrighteous wealth. They may have been engaged in unrighteous activities. Their family may have been gained wealth contrary to God's Instructions for Economic Life.

New Christians with unrighteous wealth should give it away immediately, but this often does not happen. A common temptation is to say, "I will keep my unrighteous wealth, but I will use it for God's purposes". Christian leaders will often agree with this temptation because they have some works that need financial support. This temptation is wrong for two reasons.

The gospels say that unrighteous wealth should be given to the poor. They never say that unrighteous wealth should be used to support Christian ministries. Support for Christian ministries should come through relationships, not by redirecting unrighteous wealth.

Spiritual Control

Unrighteous wealth is not neutral. Christians who retain it will be corrupted by the unrighteous spirit that clings to it. A spiritual power called Finance works through unrighteous wealth.

> You cannot serve God and mammon (Luke 16:13).

Mammon was the Aramaic name of this spiritual force, but today it would be better called Finance.

Unrighteous wealth also carries a spirit of greed. A new believer will need to get free from these spirits if they have controlled their lives. People who hold onto their unrighteous wealth, give these spirits access to their lives, which leaves them vulnerable to evil. They will be caught in an endless power struggle between their new master and their old master.

The only way to escape the spirits attached to unrighteous wealth is to give it away. This is why Jesus said it is hard for rich people to enter his Kingdom (Luke 18:25) and James warned that clinging to unrighteous wealth leads to disaster (James 5:1-5).

Wealth gained unrighteously is of no value to God, but it can be a big burden for a new Christian. They must get rid of it, so they can receive the true gifts that Jesus has for them. The Pharisees could not accept Jesus' teaching.

> The Pharisees, who loved money, heard all this and were sneering at Jesus (Luke 16:14).

Their refusal to deal with unrighteous wealth was a dangerous mistake. They missed out on the spiritual blessings that the Holy Spirit released to people like Barnabas who obeyed Jesus and gave their unrighteous wealth away.

Revolutionary Issue

Unrighteous wealth is a huge issue for the modern church. In the last century, millions of people in the western world have come to faith. This should have resulted in a massive continuous jubilee, as the new Christians gave away their unrighteous wealth, but this has not happened. The consequences are serious.

- The poor have been robbed of blessing.
- The gospel has been hindered.
- Unrighteous wealth has been stored up for judgment.

The jubilee of giving has not occurred because the church has taught the false doctrine of tithing and ignored Jesus' teaching about giving away unrighteous wealth. It has taught Christians that if they tithe on the income from their unrighteous wealth, it does not need to be given away. "Share your unrighteous gains with the church and it will be fine" is a useful teaching. Very few churches have taught that unrighteous wealth must be given away, so Jesus' teaching has been ignored.

The consequence is that the church has robbed the poor. The church has gained a tenth of the income from unrighteous wealth, and the poor have got nothing. This is not quite what Jesus had in mind. It means that a significant proportion of the property of God's people is unrighteous wealth. If we are open to the Holy Spirit, we will realise that they hold more unrighteous wealth than we knew. This will have to be given away to bring his full blessing.

If only a few of Gods people understood the meaning of unrighteous wealth and acted on Jesus' teaching in obedience to the Spirit, it would start a revolution.

5

Giving and Sharing

Kingdom Community

As the gospel advances, neighbourhood churches will develop into Kingdom Communities, led by elders who love Jesus. The people of the community will be bound together by love for Jesus and a commitment to serving each other. They will love and support everyone living within their neighbourhood, including those who have rejected the gospel.

All activities in a Kingdom Community will be governed by Jesus' command to love one another, as he loved us. Giving and sharing of the goods and services will be normal within a Kingdom Community, as people will be bound together by love. Love keeps no record of giving, so people will not record what they owe each other. Instead, people will try to outdo each other in showing love (Romans 12:9-18). They will share gladly.

Contribute to the needs of the Lord's people (Rom 12:13).

The Greek word for "contribute" is "koinoneo", which also means "distribute" or "share". It is linked to "koinonia", the word for fellowship that is also used for the "communion" of the Lord's Supper.

People in a Kingdom Community will give to those in need because they love Jesus. They will share what they have because Jesus loves them and they love each other.

Love is the key to community. If people love each other, giving and sharing gets easier. But love is not easy. Some communities will have learned to love, so giving and sharing will be normal. Other communities will be still struggling to love, so giving and sharing will be less common. Love does not demand giving and sharing. People learning to love must not be put under pressure to give or share.

All gifts must be must motivated by love and without strings attached. People with a surplus must not use gifts to manipulate or control those in need by imposing conditions on them.

No Pressure

Giving and sharing are an expression of love, not a rule to be imposed. God's people are always permitted to buy and sell (see chapter 10). Elders must not put pressure on people to give. They must be free to sell what they have produced rather than give it away. They are entitled to be compensated for their efforts, so they must be able to take payment without any condemnation if they choose. Forcing people to give or serve against their will is theft.

People serving within a community will often need some income, so it should never be assumed that they will work for nothing. They should be offered payment for what they do and allowed to decide if they will take it. Those whom Jesus has set free must not be pressured into giving to others.

When payment is made for goods and services within the community, the process will be different from the wider world. A buyer will not try to bid the price down as low as possible, but will offer what it is worth to them, or what the seller might need. A seller will not demand a top price but take account of what the buyer can afford. Paying a generous price is a good way to give.

The story of Ananias and Sapphire is well known, but a key lesson from the incident is that giving must be voluntary.

> Ananias, how is it that Satan has so filled your heart that you have lied to the Holy Spirit and have kept for yourself some of the money you received for the land? Didn't it belong to you before it was sold? And after it was sold, wasn't the money at your disposal (Acts 5:3-4)?

Ananias's land belonged to him before he sold it. The money belonged to him after he had sold it. He was under no compulsion to give anything. He should have been able to keep the entire value of the property for himself without facing any condemnation.

Sharing in a Kingdom Community must always be a response to the love of Jesus. The motivation must be compassion, not condemnation. Demanding that someone share is unacceptable. When people are willing to love each other, leaders must not use their commitment to control them.

Between Communities

A Kingdom Community will not be self-sufficient, so even if it has diverse skills and giftings, participants will not be able to get everything they need from within it. They will need goods and services produced in other communities and the outside world. Groups of people will work together within a Kingdom Community to produce things needed by other communities.

The flow of goods and services flow between communities will be a mix of giving and sharing and buying and selling, depending on the relationships between them. Some surplus goods will be given without expecting payment. However, there will be many situations when payment is appropriate. If the production process is complicated, they will need to sell some of their output to purchase raw materials and equipment. They will not be looking for big profits but seeking opportunities to bless other people. They will listen to the Spirit and decide when to accept payment.

Kingdom Communities must never be shut away from the world as their witness would be lost. Some followers of Jesus will travel outside their community to work in paid employment. Some will trade with the outside world to obtain the benefits of specialisation. Others will be led by the Spirit into the world to give and serve.

Love one another is the standard for followers of Jesus, so giving and sharing will become normal as they learn to be led by the Holy Spirit. God has a different standard for the people of the world. They will sometimes share, but they will mostly sell their surplus. God is satisfied if the people of the world avoid stealing when they buy and sell to each other.

Serving Each Other

In the modern world, many community functions have been commercialised and commodified. Once, childcare was shared with grandparents and others in the village. These days childcare is a business and care is purchased for a fee. The same is true of education. Aged care used to be provided by families and neighbours, but now care is provided by commercial rest homes. Most food is now bought, whereas once it was grown within the community and shared. Security, cleaning and gardening are new services that are now purchased from a market provider.

As Kingdom Communities are strengthened by the gospel, many services that are bought and sold will become opportunities for giving and sharing within a community that is bound together by love. People within a community will share their gifts and skills, reducing the need for money transactions.

A Kingdom Community will be like a big family. Goods and services are exchanged within a family by giving and sharing. Parents feed and clothe their children not expecting anything in return. Children care for their parents and other elderly relatives. Buying and selling between family members will be very rare. Members of the family will be committed to caring for each other. Sharing is the strength of families. The same will be true of Kingdom Communities.

Body Love

The members of a Kingdom Community have been baptised into one body.

> Even so the body is not made up of one part but of many (1 Cor 12:14).

The members of the body of Jesus are dependent on each other.

> Now if the foot should say, "Because I am not a hand, I do not belong to the body," it would not for that reason stop being part of the body (1 Cor 12:15).

The hand cannot say to the foot, your pain does not affect me, so I do not care about it.

> If one part suffers, every part suffers with it (1 Cor 12:26).

If a foot is suffering, every member of the body should feel its pain.

The eye who has a professional salary cannot say to the hand that has lost its income, your suffering does not affect me. The ear that has a family inheritance cannot say that it is not affected by the leg with a disability. This is why John said,

> If anyone has material possessions and sees a brother or sister in need but has no pity on them, how can the love of God be in that person (1 John 3:17)?

If one member of a body of believers has worldly wealth, and another is suffering in poverty, the love that Jesus requires is missing.

> This is how we know what love is: Jesus Christ laid down his life for us. And we ought to lay down our lives for our brothers and sisters (1 John 3:16)?

If love is working, caring and sharing will be effective. People will not be able to stay in poverty for long. A community that gives and shares can live in plenty without needing abundant material wealth.

Taking Advantage

Some of the people of the neighbourhood might take advantage of generosity that pervades a Kingdom Community. Jesus explained that it is normal for generosity to be ripped off. He expects his followers to respond with even greater generosity.

> Bless those who curse you, pray for those who mistreat you.
> Do good to them without expecting to get anything back (Luke 6:28,35).

> If you suffer as a follower of Christ, do not be ashamed, but praise God that you bear that name (1 Pet 4:16).

Being ripped off is an opportunity to imitate Jesus by blessing those who take advantage of us.

> Love keeps no record of wrongs (1 Cor 13:5).

Followers of Jesus should respond to those who abuse their kindness by showing even greater love and generosity. We are all freeloaders on Jesus. We benefit from his death on the cross by accepting full salvation without contributing anything towards the cost. Jesus does not object, but all his followers have taken something for nothing from him. We have benefitted from his love without giving much in return.

The people of a Kingdom Community will combine their resources to provide services that will benefit everyone living in their neighbourhood. They might ask for voluntary contributions from those who will benefit. Many people will support their initiatives and choose to contribute (Rom 13:7-8).

However, some people will not be able to afford the cost. Others will deliberately decide to freeload. This is not a problem as it provides an opportunity for followers of Jesus to demonstrate practical love and generosity. Some will choose to contribute extra to cover those who cannot afford to pay. Others will pay extra to make up for any who refuse to pay.

When people living on the edge of a Kingdom Community accept the benefits offered without giving anything back, it becomes an opportunity to show love. Jesus said,

> If someone forces you to go one mile, go with him two miles (Matt 5:41).

The soldier who forces someone to carry his pack for a mile wants a service without paying for it. We should not resist those abusing our generosity, but express love by giving them more than they expect. Jesus' response to those who take advantage of his kindness is abundant generosity.

> Uphold the weak, be patient with everyone. See that no one renders evil for evil to anyone, but always pursue what is good both for yourselves and for all. Rejoice always (1 Thes 5:14-16).

6

True Wealth

Followers of Jesus should have a different attitude to wealth. We should not worry about our lives and what to eat and drink.

> Do not worry about your life, what you will eat or drink; or about your body, what you will wear. Is not life more important than food, and the body more important than clothes... O you of little faith? So do not worry, saying, 'What shall we eat?' or 'What shall we drink?' or 'What shall we wear?' For the pagans run after all these things, and your heavenly Father knows that you need them (Matt 6:25,31,32).

For most of Jesus' listeners, the daily battle for survival was a relentless struggle. How could they stop worrying about food, when hunger was only a few hours away? Jesus suggested a different approach to life.

> Seek first the kingdom of God and his righteousness, and all these things will be given to you as well. Therefore, do not worry about tomorrow, for tomorrow will worry about itself. Each day has enough trouble of its own (Matt 6:33,34).

This message was jarring for Jesus' listeners. Most were totally worried about what they would eat tomorrow. By stopping to listen to Jesus, they had probably missed an opportunity to earn tomorrow's food. The idea that they could stop worrying about tomorrow seemed absurd.

Yet the people who followed Jesus in Acts 2 and 4 experienced this becoming a reality.

There were no needy persons among them (Acts 4:34)

This was not the result of gold coins falling from the sky.

They shared everything they had (Acts 4:32)

Believers no longer had to worry about what they would eat tomorrow because they shared with each other.

Most modern Christians do not have to worry about what they will eat tomorrow. We tend to assume that Jesus' teaching means that people who seek God's Kingdom will prosper, but that is not what he meant at all.

When we follow Jesus, we choose a new king. A king owns all the property within his kingdom. He assigns property to his followers, but they only hold it while they remain in his favour. People who oppose the king will have their property confiscated.

When Christians choose to "seek the kingdom", all their possessions become the property of their king. Giving a tenth of what they own is not an option. Everything they own now belongs to Jesus and must be used as he directs. This produced the change of thinking recorded in the Acts of the Apostles (cf Luke 12:22).

No one **claimed** that any of his possessions was his own (Acts 4:32)

This was not unusual behaviour, but the normal response of people giving allegiance to a new king.

Seeking the Kingdom first means surrendering all our income and wealth to Jesus and using it as the Holy Spirit directs. If he tells us to sell our property and give it away, that is what we must do. It no longer belongs to us, but to our king. If the Holy Spirit tells us to share our possessions then we have no option. Reading Acts, it seems that the Holy Spirit likes telling people to share, so we should not be surprised if he asks us to do the same.

Counting the Cost

Jesus warned his listeners to count the cost, before choosing to follow him (Luke 14:26-32). A king who goes into battle without working out if he has enough troops to win is stupid. Jesus illustrated this choice with reference to money and wealth.

> So then, none of you can be my disciple who does not give
> up all his own possessions. Therefore, salt is good; but if
> even salt has become tasteless, with what will it be seasoned
> (Luke 14:33-34)?

The cost we have to count is real. To be a disciple of Jesus, we must give up all our possessions. The Greek word for "give up" is "apossetai". It means "renounce" or "say goodbye". Those who follow Jesus must "say goodbye" to their possessions. They might still be there, but we no longer own them. They belong to Jesus, so the Holy Spirit can use them as he wills.

Giving up our possessions changes our questions of Jesus. We should not ask, "Can I buy a new television?" Rather we should be asking the Holy Spirit different questions. "What do you want to do with the money in the bank account that has my name on it.?" "What do you want to do with the wealth that used to belong to me?" If we asked these questions, we might be surprised at what the Spirit would ask. If we don't ask these questions, we will be like salt that has lost its flavour (Luke 14:34). If we are not willing to say goodbye to our possessions, we cannot expect to influence a culture that is obsessed with wealth.

Many Christians respond to Jesus' teaching by asking, "Can a Christian own property?" The New Testament answer is "No". Christians cannot own property. The reason we cannot own property is that we have a king. Once we give allegiance to King Jesus, all our property belongs to him. We cannot own property because everything we have is his.

The Holy Spirit may tell people to use their property for a particular purpose. He told Joanna, the wife of Cuza, Susanna; and several other women to use their property to support Jesus.

> These women were helping to support them out of their
> own means (Luke 8:3).

These women held onto their property as stewards, but the Holy Spirit prompted them to use it to support Jesus and his disciples. In the same way, the Holy Spirit told Joseph of Arimathea to pay for Jesus to be buried (Matt 27:57-58).

The answer to every question about property is simple. Jesus owns it all. He may allow us to hold some of his property as stewards, but we cannot call it our own. Good stewards use his property as the Holy Spirit directs. The answer to all questions about property is to obey the Holy Spirit.

Human Heart

Jesus understood the human heart.

> For where your treasure is, there your heart will be also (Luke 12:34).

Humans tend to focus on the place where their treasure is kept. If our treasure is in a bank, we will focus on the size of our account. Jesus does not want us to be distracted, so we must store our treasure in heaven.

The main reason that people store up wealth is to provide security for the future. Jesus ruled this out when he told us to trust God for the future.

> Do not worry about tomorrow, for tomorrow will worry about itself. Each day has enough trouble of its own (Matt 6:34).

Storing wealth for security in the future is pointless, as no earthly store is safe. Corrupt bankers will steal it, or monetary inflation will slowly eat it away. Wealth is always fragile.

> Do not wear yourself out to get rich;
> do not trust your own cleverness.
> Cast but a glance at riches, and they are gone,
> for they will surely sprout wings (Prov 23:4-5).

In troubled times wealth shrivels up, and those who trust it for their security will be disappointed.

> Wealth is worthless in the day of wrath, but righteousness delivers from death (Prov 11:4).

Jesus did not pretend that the future will be free of problems. He knew that we would face trials, but he told us to prepare by storing up treasures in heaven (Luke 12:33).

> Store up for yourselves treasures in heaven...where thieves do not break in and steal (Matt 6:20).

Building up wealth on earth is risky. Unexpected events can destroy it. Real security comes from treasure in heaven.

> Treasures of wickedness profit nothing,
> But righteousness delivers from death (Prov 10:2).

Unacceptable Teaching

Jesus' teaching about security seems impractical in the modern world. Our security is based on treasure on earth. We have superannuation funds for our retirement. We have insurance to protect us against the risk of crisis. We keep a nest egg in the bank for use in an emergency. Not only are these things treasure on earth, but they tie up resources that could be used by God.

Jesus says that we should not need these things, but we would not feel secure without them. We have this dilemma because we have not understood what Jesus was saying. He explained why we should not need treasure on earth for our security.

> Do not be afraid, little flock, for your Father has been
> pleased to give you the kingdom (Luke 12:32)

The reason that we should not be scared is that Jesus gives his kingdom to a "little flock". The disciples would not need treasure on earth because this little flock would become their treasure. They would not need wealth for security because they would care for each other. A little flock can love and support each other.

Caring and sharing in the body of Jesus is the best source of security. The early Christians said goodbye to their property (Acts 4:32-33). They stopped referring to their property as their own because they were united in love. Giving and sharing were normal. The result was "no needy persons among them".

Resources that were previously tied up in personal security were no longer needed because the body of Jesus was their security. The gospel of the kingdom had transformed their lives so much that they felt secure in the love of the believers around them. They did not need life insurance or superannuation because sharing had made them unnecessary.

Better Solution

Modern Christians are uneasy when they hear Jesus' teaching about treasure in heaven, but we have missed the point. Trying to stop worrying about tomorrow is impossible if we don't belong to a "little flock" that is receiving the Kingdom. People who belong to a little flock do not need storehouses on earth.

The Kingdom comes first. Obeying Jesus' teaching about wealth is not practical in the modern world because we live as individuals. We are not "all together in the same place" (Acts 2:44). We still consider our property our own. We do not give to everyone who has a need. We are not part of a little flock that loves each other, so we need insurance, superannuation and money in the bank.

The solution is to "Seek the Kingdom of God first". When we get serious about the Kingdom, we will sell our property and move closer to the little flock we are part of. Once we are together in one place, we will be able to share and care for each other. When sharing and caring are normal, we will find that we do not need insurance or a nest egg in the bank. Instead of storing money to provide for ourselves in a day of trouble, we will be saving to help others in their day of trouble. Treasure on earth will be irrelevant because we have the real treasure in a Kingdom Community.

The Modern Problem

The big problem eating the heart out of our modern culture is the collapse of community. Industrialisation, globalisation and urbanisation have eliminated the links between people that once held society together. Family members can travel all over the world to live and work. People and families live in isolation.

The collapse of community is greatest in modern cities, where migration and urbanisation have broken down traditional connections. Social mobility prevents stable relationships from developing, and family life is breaking down. People become cogs in the corporate machine and life is characterised by loneliness and personal insecurity.

Modern suburban culture creates barriers to communication and encourages individualism. As communities are breaking down and fear is rising, high fences are going up between houses isolating people from each other. This isolation means that most people do not belong to the community where they live.

To restore cohesion to our societies, real community will have to be restored to our societies, but it is not clear who will do it.

Politicians have an inbuilt tendency to push power and money to the top, which always weakens society.

The church should be strengthening the foundations of society, but this is not happening. The early Christians were "all together in one place", but modern Christians drive to church, just as they drive to work and to shop. The church is almost as fragmented as the rest of society. This is sad, because followers of Jesus are supposed to be experts on fellowship and loving one another.

The collapse of community and our fragmented lifestyle prevents us from living out Jesus' teaching on money. We have to build up treasures on earth because we are not part of Kingdom Communities that could support us in time of trouble. We do not have relationships with followers of Jesus committed to providing financial support for each other. Isolated Christians have no choice but to fend for themselves by storing up treasure on earth.

Different Order

Acts 2 provides a solution to our isolation. The early church was altogether in one place, so they sold their possessions and property. In the modern world, the antidote is the same, but the order is the other way around. Our problem is that suburban property prevents us from being together. The solution is

Selling their property and possessions (Acts 2:45).
Once Christians are willing to sell their properties, they will be able to move closer to the other Christians that they relate to.

All the believers were in one place (Acts 2:44)
This is the ultimate goal. We must be together, so that we can love each other, as Jesus loved us.

Some of those who sell their houses to move closer to other Christians will be selling down. This will release a surplus that can be used to provide financial support for helping the poor.

They were sharing them with all, as anyone might have need (Acts 2:45).
When Christians live closer to each other, serious sharing becomes a practical alternative.

This radical change will not happen by accident. Locality-based apostles working street by street, neighbourhood by neighbourhood can change our societies from the bottom up. I describe how this process should work in my book Being Church Where We Live.

In Kingdom Communities, giving and sharing will be a normal way of obtaining things from other people. People will love one another by giving their surplus to people who need it. Everyone will try to have something that they can share with others.

True Wealth

True wealth is our relationship with the body of Jesus. If a little flock of believers is committed to loving me, as Jesus loved us, then I have amazing security. Their love and commitment provide better security for the future than money in a bank. Money in a bank can be lost or stolen, but love never fails.

> Love always protects, always trusts, always hopes, always perseveres. Love never fails. (1 Cor 13:7-8).

The best security comes from being loved by a body of people who are committed to serving and supporting each other. Fear of the future makes us rely on wealth.

> There is no fear in love. But perfect love drives out fear (1 John 4:18).

John was speaking about the love of God, but this also relates to love of another. If we love one another, fear has no place.

The apostle Paul's bank account was empty, but he explained in his letter to the Philippians that he was content. He trusted in God to supply what he needed.

> My God will meet all your needs according to the riches of his glory in Christ Jesus (Phil 4:19).

He trusted God, but he knew that God could work through the people who loved him.

> I have more than enough. I am amply supplied, now that I have received the gifts you sent. They are a fragrant offering, an acceptable sacrifice, pleasing to God (Phil 4:18).

Paul's wealth was in heaven, but it was delivered to him by people who loved him.

7

Equality

In a modern economy, inequality is normal. Honest markets often produce unequal outcomes. People with wealth get a head start while those born in poverty fall behind. People who make wise business decisions usually prosper. Those who invent innovative new products become rich quite quickly.

People are sometimes "ripped off" by bad people, but often poverty is an outcome of the trials of life. People often make bad decisions that make them worse off. A few make serious mistakes that push them and their children into poverty.

- Wealth flows to those who already have wealth.
- Bad decisions can produce a huge loss.
- People with rare skills often get higher pay than others.
- People who do not use their skills wisely can find themselves in poverty.
    Lazy hands make a man poor (Prov 10:4).
- People born into poverty will usually struggle to escape.
- The sick and handicapped often suffer financially.
- People can be harmed when people they trust make mistakes.
- Employees suffer from the errors of their employers.
- During economic depressions, the poor suffer the most.
- People caught up in a war usually lose everything.

- Droughts, tornadoes and floods push people into poverty.

The vagaries of life produce inequality, even if everyone is honest.

Equality

God's goal is equity. Joshua divided the land equally among families of Israel.

> Joshua cast lots for them in Shiloh in the presence of the Lord, and he distributed the land to the Israelites according to their tribal divisions (Joshua 18:10).

The jubilee ensured the land continued to be equally distributed.

When the Israelites gathered manna, some gathered more than others, but each one got what they needed.

> The Israelites did as they were told; some gathered much, some little. And when they measured it by the omer, the one who gathered much did not have too much, and the one who gathered little did not have too little. Everyone had gathered just as much as they needed (Ex 16:17-18).

God ensured that everyone got enough with no one getting ahead at the expense of others.

Jesus confirmed the importance of equality in his parable about the Vineyard Workers. Workers who worked for only the last hour were paid the same as those who worked for the entire day.

> They began to grumble against the landowner… These who were hired last worked only one hour and **you have made them equal** to us who have borne the burden of the work and the heat of the day (Matt 20:11-12).

This employer had promised to pay "whatever is right". Jesus explained that actions to increase equality are right (dikaion).

Paul continued this push for equality in his letters.

> Our desire is… that there might be equality (2 Cor 8:13).

This is a radical vision. Paul believed that obedience to Jesus and God's Instructions for Economic Life would produce equality.

God's Way

God's objective is equality, but his solution is surprising. He will not force people to be good, so he does not require compulsory redistribution of incomes. The New Testament does not support

taxation to transfer wealth from the rich to the poor. This just makes the rich angry, while the poor remain poor.

God's solution to inequality is effective because it does not require force or coercion but relies on love and compassion. Life in Kingdom Communities will be very different from life in the world.

> Our desire is not that others might be relieved while you are hard pressed, but that there might be equality. At the present time your plenty will supply what they need, so that in turn their plenty will supply what you need. Then there will be equality (2 Cor 8:13-14).

God expects people with plenty to give generously to those who are hard pressed. He expects those who have prospered to show compassion for those who have not done so well. Serious giving and sharing will increase equality.

Paul is not writing about compulsory redistribution, but generosity and sharing.

> For I testify that they gave as much as they were able, and even beyond their ability. Entirely on their own, they urgently pleaded with us for the privilege of sharing in this service to the saints. And they did not do as we expected, but they gave themselves first to the Lord and then to us in keeping with God's will (2 Cor 8:3-5).

Paul knew that if followers of Jesus captured this sharing concept, the result would be equality. We are a long way from Paul's vision, because we have not understood that sharing is the normal response to Jesus death on the cross. Generous sharing should be normal in Kingdom Communities. Some people will still earn more than they need, but they will not keep it for themselves. Their blessing will benefit everyone.

> He who gathered much did not have too much, and he who gathered little did not have too little (2 Cor 8:15).

Followers of Jesus will have a radically different attitude to possessions. Instead of being something to enjoy, they will be seen as a gift from God to strengthen the body of Jesus.

> All the believers were one in heart and mind. No one claimed that any of his possessions was his own, but they shared everything they had. With great power the apostles

continued to testify to the resurrection of the Lord Jesus,
and much grace was upon them all. There were no needy
persons among them (Acts 4:32-34).

Flowing grace and love produced a society with no needy people.

Jesus Prophecy

Jesus was blunter than Paul. When teaching his disciples, he
promised that the natural order of things would be turned upside
down.

> Blessed are you who are poor,
> for yours is the kingdom of God.
> Blessed are you who hunger now,
> for you will be satisfied (Luke 6:20-21).

Jesus promised that the poor would receive the Kingdom of God,
but his message to the rich was a shock.

> Woe to you who are rich,
> for you have already received your comfort.
> Woe to you who are well fed now,
> for you will go hungry (Luke 6:24-25).

Jesus warned that the people who are rich and well fed would lose
their comfort and be hungry.

Before Jesus was born, Mary had prophesied a massive
economic and political upheaval.

> He has performed mighty deeds with his arm...
> He has lifted up the humble.
> He has filled the hungry with good things
> but has sent the rich away empty (Luke 1:51-53).

Those who are poor will be lifted up and be made comfortable.
The rich and powerful will be disappointed.

These prophecies will not be achieved by war and revolution.
They will be fulfilled voluntarily through giving and sharing. They
were fulfilled by the early church, but they are not often fulfilled in
the modern world.

The prophecies of Jesus and Mary are a challenge to the church.
If the gospel is being preached effectively, the poor and hungry
should be being lifted up and being satisfied. This will happen
when followers of Jesus heed the Instructions for Economic Life.

Jesus Jubilee

At the beginning of his ministry, Jesus announced a new jubilee.

> The Spirit of the Lord is on me,
> because he has anointed me
> to proclaim good news to the poor.
> He has sent... to set the oppressed free,
> to proclaim the year of the Lord's favour (Luke 4:18-19).

Jesus promised that his jubilee would be good news for the poor. It would provide new freedom for people who were oppressed by the trials of life.

We tend to spiritualise this promise, but Jesus' words created an immense expectation for his listeners. They expected the deliverance that he promised. Jesus was not promising to overthrow the Romans and ascend to David's throne in Jerusalem. That would not be practical. He was not even advocating forced re-distribution of land back to the boundaries laid out by Joshua. That was not possible while the people controlling the land were protected by Roman privilege.

Jesus announced a completely different jubilee. It would transform economic life in the villages of Galilee and Judea, as people applied the Instructions for Economic Life. The land laws might not be practical, but all the other instructions were still relevant and they did not need government intervention or consent. They could be applied by ordinary people, despite Roman control. Application of the Instructions for Economic Life would transform their society as practical sharing and caring were restored.

Village Restoration

The people of Israel were looking for a Messiah who would deliver them from the Romans. Jesus' approach was different. He intended to renew economic life from the ground up. Most people still lived in villages. By applying the Instructions for Economic Life, they could strengthen their village communities. The most dramatic change would come when wealthy people gave away their unrighteous wealth.

Under the pressure of economic hardship, the people had given up on the Instructions for Economic Life and stopped caring for each other. Most were so busy struggling to survive that they had no time to think about the pain of others. Caring and sharing had stopped and everyone looked out for themselves.

Cheating and stealing to get ahead were normal, as people assumed that they had no other choice. Jesus challenged this view. He wanted the people to see that they would be better off if they adopted God's way of living.

Jesus spent most of his time in the villages of Galilee, challenging the people to restore the old way of life as prescribed in the Instructions for Economic Life. When he sent his disciples out on a mission, he told them to go to a village and stay with a person of peace. Their aim was not just to get converts, but to restore village communities to God's model for economic life.

The disciples were to focus on the person of influence, or the person of peace because this person would be important for changing the way that people lived. The gospel and the Instructions for Economic Life could restore the economic strength of village life and transform them into Kingdom Communities.

The villages were a great place to re-learn giving and sharing. The disciples took no money with them, so they would be dependent on giving and sharing for their survival. They would give the villagers healing and deliverance from evil spirits. The people of the village would give them food and shelter. The experience would show them the benefit of giving and sharing as required by the Instructions for Economic Life.

Jesus did not confront the Romans directly. He introduced subtle changes at the village level where they would not notice the challenge. The Romans could not stop this jubilee, as Jesus' Kingdom would spread unnoticed like yeast through dough.

> The kingdom of heaven is like yeast that a woman took and mixed into about sixty pounds of flour until it worked all through the dough (Matt 13:33).

Yeast cannot be seen, but it transforms flour so that when it is kneaded, it turns into dough ready to be baked. The pressure of the kneading makes the yeast more effective.

The parable explains that the Kingdom of God will be established as the gospel and the Spirit spread from village to village restoring economic life. Like yeast in dough, most of the change would not be visible to the Roman authorities. Their pressure would make the Instructions for Economic Life more effective.

Jesus also warned about a different type of yeast.
> Be careful. Be on your guard against the yeast of the Pharisees and Sadducees (Matt 16:6).

The Pharisees and the Sadducees ignored the Instructions for Economic Life. Instead, they collaborated with the Romans to protect their position and privilege. Jesus later warned that those who had collaborated with the Romans would be destroyed. The collaboration system would be swept away (Matt 24). When that happened, the centre of economic life would shift to the villages that had prepared by applying the Instructions for Economic Life. By adopting them, they could even survive in exile.

The New Testament does not record what happened in Galilee and Judea as a result of Jesus' teaching as it focused on events of his life. Given that the people wanted to make him king, it can be assumed that the impact was dramatic. Some rich people would have discovered that all their wealth was unrighteous. If they chose to follow Jesus' teaching and give away their unrighteous wealth, they would find themselves "empty" as Mary had warned, but they would have a new group of neighbours and "one anothers".

The early church carried on practising the Instructions for Economic Life after Jesus had ascended. People like Barnabas sold their unrighteous wealth and gave it to those in need.
> They sold property and possessions to give to anyone who had need (Acts 2:.45).

The church provided food and care for widows, orphans and others who were poor (Acts 6:1). Paul built on this with teaching about caring for widows (1 Tim 5:3-15). The followers of Jesus provided clothing for people in need.
> In Joppa, there was a disciple named Tabitha (in Greek her name is Dorcas); she was always doing good and helping the poor. All the widows stood around, crying and showing him the robes and other clothing that Dorcas had made (Acts 9:36-39).

Dorcas was raised from the dead, but the incident also reminds us that Christians continued to provide for people in need, as required by the Instructions for Economic Life. Their motivation was love, but the instructions put shape around the practice of love.

Jesus promised his followers who had left everything to follow him that they would receive farms and houses in the current age.

> No one who has left home or brothers or sisters or mother or father or children or fields for me and the gospel will fail to receive a hundred times as much in this present age: homes, brothers, sisters, mothers, children and fields (Mark 10:29-30).

This inheritance of land and houses would be the outcome of Jesus' jubilee as people gave away their unrighteous wealth.

When God's people take the Instructions for Economic Life seriously and deal with unrighteous wealth by giving it away, a dramatic jubilee will occur. Wealth will flow from the rich to the poor.

If followers of Jesus share and care for each other, communities will be strengthened. Paul confirmed this in his letter to Timothy.

> Command those who are rich in this present world not to be arrogant nor to put their hope in wealth, which is so uncertain, but to put their hope in God, who richly provides us with everything for our enjoyment. Command them to do good, to be rich in good deeds, and to be generous and willing to share. In this way they will lay up treasures for themselves as a firm foundation (1 Tim 6:17-19).

If Christians applied the jubilee that Jesus commanded, an amazing economic transformation would occur.

If the modern church took Jesus' teaching on unrighteous wealth seriously, there would be a huge flood of giving just as Jesus announced. Unfortunately, we tend to spiritualise Jesus' teaching on unrighteous wealth, so the poor continue to be hungry and the rich do fine.

8
Debt

Debt is a major cause of inequality in the modern world. A heavy burden of debt weighs down people and businesses. Most of the money loaned is unrighteous wealth that needs to be given away.

Household Debt

In the western world, households carry a massive burden of debt. Working households are now taking on unprecedented debt to purchase their homes. The price of a house is whatever a bank will lend to a purchaser. Banks will lend families as much debt as they can afford to pay interest on over their lifetime.

Most households take on a mortgage close to the limit of what they can afford to pay. This means that the price of houses drifts up to a level at which most families can only just afford to pay the interest on their mortgage. Families often spend more than half of their income on mortgage payments. Most will pay for their house two or three times over in interest. Families are willing to take on these massive debts because they hope to make a capital gain on their property.

Banks can create money as long as they can find people to borrow (see chapter 16). This expansion of lending causes families to bid up house prices, fulfilling their desire for capital gains. Property prices usually increase faster than everything else, which allows households to take on even more debt.

The effect of this increase is that households end up with the same stock of housing, but with huge additional debt. The growth of housing debt shifts tremendous wealth to the banks. If borrowing such large amounts was unacceptable, the price of houses would fall dramatically. Households would have much less debt, but they would still own the same number of dwellings.

On top of their housing debt, most families will take a loan to buy a motor vehicle. The better-educated will have education loans to repay. These debts are a burden for much of their lives.

Poorer households have hire purchase loans for their televisions, furniture and motor vehicles. Really poor families will often have additional debt to loan sharks and pay-day lenders.

Debt is a huge burden on modern families. As real wages have declined, struggling families have increased their debt in an attempt to maintain their lost lifestyle. They are reduced to a lifetime as slaves of debt.

Debt is a claim on future income. People in debt live with the constant fear that a crisis will prevent them from earning sufficient income to repay their debt, as this would plunge them into deeper poverty. If the lender forecloses on the loan, they might lose all their assets and enter a life of destitution.

Business Debt

In recent decades, businesses have vastly increased their debt. Economists have suggested that increasing debt is just as efficient as increasing equity. Many businesses have taken this bad advice and chosen to carry extra debt so that the owners do not need to make an additional capital injection. They have ignored the problem that during a downturn, debt is fixed, whereas equity changes to reflect the actual value of the business. Interest still has to be paid, while dividends can be withheld.

In the big business world, hedge funds and private equity firms have purchased many businesses using borrowed funds to pay for the shares. These leveraged buy-outs replace share equity and dividends with debt and interest payments. Surplus assets are usually extracted and replaced with debt.

Developing Countries

People in poor countries are often weighed down with back-breaking debt. The burden has been compounded in recent years, as western banks have rapidly expanded their loans to businesses and governments in developing countries. This results in huge payments of interest to foreign banks. Paying this interest is a drain on the income and wealth of people who are already poor.

Debt industry

Increasing dependence on debt has allowed finance to become the largest sector in many economies. It is usually called the finance, insurance and real estate sector, but I refer to it as the debt industry. In modern developed economies, the debt industry typically earns nearly a third of all corporate profits.

Households and businesses pay a steady stream of interest to the banks that dominate the debt industry. However, the debt industry doesn't just make loans and collect interest. It slices up debt and repackages it into a range of financial derivatives, such as credit default swaps and mortgage-backed securities and various forms of collateralised debt obligations. The debt industry claims to be shifting risk to those who can bear it, but the global financial crisis showed that no one knew who held the risk.

Banks and their lawyers charge a fee or commission each time one of these debt instruments is created and every time one is traded. Trade in these debt instruments is enormous, so these commissions are a huge source of income for the debt industry. The people who create, sell and manage this chopped-up and re-packaged debt earn huge salaries.

Increased debt and financialisation have created a massive invisible infrastructure that sits on top of the real economy and sucks income and wealth out of it. A network of ever-growing interest-bearing claims has been wrapped around the productive sector, making businesses less competitive.

This debt industry produces nothing of real value. It syphons away business profits, leaving less for the payment of wages and salaries to employees. It drains away a significant share of family income and transfers it to those who are already wealthy. It cripples the poor and strengthens those who have plenty. The income of the debt industry is mostly unrighteous wealth.

Excessive debt and trade in debt caused the global financial crisis. The debt industry was not wiped out, as in previous economic crises. The leaders of the debt sector have significant control over democratic governments, so they ensured that banks were bailed out while families and businesses bore the burden.

Much of the bad debt was not written off but sold to central banks. New debt is now building up on top of this already unwieldy structure of debt. A crisis will inevitably come when people realise that the volume of debt is too large to be repaid.

Governments usually feed inflation to liquidate the debt that constrains the economy. However, wages and pensions do not keep up with inflation, so the poor lose ground, while wealthy debtors benefit.

Legal Protection

Modern legal systems favour creditors over debtors. Government courts and the agents enforce debt contracts on behalf of creditors and attempt to collect outstanding amounts, even if the debtor cannot afford it. Governments usually take the side of creditors. Their assumption is that the person who incurred the debt is responsible, even if the debt is unfair or they did not know what they were doing.

The debt industry rarely receives penalties for lending money to people that cannot afford it or charging punitive interest rates. The debtor is presumed to be at fault, so they must pay. The only escape for a debtor is to declare themselves bankrupt.

Debt is Dangerous

The Bible warns about the dangers of debt.

> The rich rule over the poor,
> and the borrower is slave to the lender (Prov 22:7).

This is not a statement of the way that things should be, but the way that they are. A borrower is a slave of the lender. While they are in debt, they have no freedom because the lender is entitled to their income and some of their assets. If disaster strikes and they cannot repay the loan, they will end up in even greater trouble. In difficult times, debts can very quickly grow large as interest arrears and late-payment penalties are added to the amount outstanding.

The Instructions for Economic Life warn poor people against offering their assets as security for a debt, as this places them in a vulnerable situation.

> Do not be one who shakes hands in pledge
> or puts up security for debts;
> if you lack the means to pay,
> your very bed will be snatched from under you (Prov 22:26-27).

Putting up security for a debt is dangerous because if things go wrong and the debt cannot be repaid, the furniture or vehicles offered as security can be lost. The Bible warns that ruthless creditors often take stuff that poor people need to live. It is not approving but explaining the way debt often develops.

Debt allows rich people to control the poor. Poor people are vulnerable, because they need to borrow, so they can be easily dominated by those who are rich. Proverbs warns rich people that oppressing the poor with debt produces unrighteous wealth.

> One who oppresses the poor to increase his wealth and one who
> gives gifts to the rich—both come to poverty (Prov 22:16).

Those who oppress the poor will lose the blessing of God.

> Do not exploit the poor because they are poor
> and do not crush the needy in court,
> for the Lord will take up their case (Prov 22:22-23).

Those who use the courts to extract debts from people that cannot afford them are fighting against God for unrighteous wealth.

Government of God

Under the Government of God, all economic transactions must be voluntary. There will be no state authority with the power to enforce debt contracts. The Instructions for Economic Life give no mechanism for making people repay their debts. This means that lenders cannot force borrowers to pay the interest they owe. They cannot force them to repay a loan. Lenders will have to rely on the goodwill of the borrower to get repaid.

Most people will repay their loans because they want to maintain a good reputation. They will realise that they might want a loan in the future and not want to spoil their credit record. They will avoid defaulting so that they continue to be trusted by the people to whom they have made promises.

Realising that they might be a creditor in the future, they will encourage the practice of repaying loans. They will set a good example for other debtors by fulfilling their commitments to repay debts. Paul urged us to repay our loans if we can.

> Give to everyone what you owe them... Let no debt remain outstanding, except the continuing debt to love one another (Rom 13:7-8).

Love requires us to repay our debts. However, this is only a moral obligation. There is no provision for enforcement of debts.

We repay our loans because we love, but love does not require us to impoverish our families. If a person cannot afford to repay a loan without plunging their family into poverty, they are not required to pay the loan.

In the Government of God, creditors lose their power, because there is no government power to enforce the repayment of loans. This shifts control from the creditor to the debtor. If the money that is owed to a lender is not repaid, there is nothing the creditor can do about it. They cannot make threats of violence to ensure repayment. Goods cannot be taken to cover the outstanding debt.

All a creditor can do is go to a judge and make their case against the person who has refused to pay the debt. Judges can confirm that a debt is owing, but they do not have authority to enforce repayment. The judge may pronounce judgement against the debtor but does not have the power to enforce their decision. They can explain their decision to the community, but public disapproval might not be enough to make the person repay the debt.

A community will only put pressure on people to repay a debt if they believe that repayment is justified. If the terms of the debt are unfair, sympathy will go to the debtor, so a creditor would make themselves unpopular by demanding repayment. The community would not support demands for penalty interest, even if the debt contract allowed it.

If a debtor is being impoverished by a debt, the judge will declare that the debt must be cancelled at the end of seven years, so the creditor will not be able to demand repayment. The judge will rule that all the interest charged must be refunded, because charging interest to a poor person is forbidden by God's law.

Judges will only support claims for the repayment of legitimate business loans. Claims by owners of unrighteous wealth for repayment of debt will not be supported by judges. They will declare that money lent by loan sharks has become unrighteous wealth that does not have to be repaid.

In God's Economy, judges applying God's law will remove the power of creditors. Courts will be reluctant to enforce many debt agreements, so repayment of debt will mostly be voluntary. Debtors will be free to walk away from their debt, because there will be no government forcing them to repay it.

Debt Decline

All lending will have to be done with an expectation that the debt might not be repaid. Lenders will develop generous debt contracts that judges would be willing to enforce. Applying God's law to repayment of loans will lead to a massive reduction in debt.

When making loans to any person or business that they do not know well, creditors will have to take into account the possibility that they might not get repaid. This uncertainty will significantly reduce the amount of lending. Lending will only be possible between people who trust each other. Big loans will disappear because the risk of loss is too great. This reluctance will significantly reduce the amount of debt in the economy.

When creditors receive the gospel, they will realise that much of their debt is unrighteous wealth that needs to be given away. The best way to give it away is to cancel the debt. Cancellation of debts will eliminate much of the debt that cripples many people.

The mountain of debt that is crushing modern economies will not be possible under the Government of God. The debt industry that sits on top of the real economy bleeding out income and wealth will wither away and disappear, as it becomes unsustainable.

Productive and Unproductive Debt

Followers of Jesus must distinguish between unproductive and productive debt. Unproductive debt is lending for consumption or property speculation. Borrowing to buy consumer goods is foolish because the borrower gets nothing extra at the end of the loan period to pay back the loan. They pay more and end up with nothing extra in return.

Speculation in real estate pushes up the price of existing properties but does not add to the stock of assets in the economy. Real estate assets produce nothing but capital gains stolen from God. Savings fed into real estate speculation that bids up prices become unproductive debt. It just enlarges the value of claims attached to existing assets, instead of producing new assets. Capital gains on real estate purchased with leveraged debt are usually unrighteous wealth. The only remedy is to cancel the debt.

Productive debt is money borrowed to buy productive assets that will make employees more productive. If the additional product earns more than the interest charges for the loan, the business is better off. The investment funded by the debt makes it more productive, so it can afford the interest payments. Debt fed into speculative activities does not increase the productive capacity of the economy, so it becomes a burden that drags it down.

In the Kingdom of God, most loans will be for business purposes. Borrowing to buy productive equipment is legitimate because productive debt produces a return that will cover the cost of the interest. However, believers will usually only borrow to get started. As God blesses them, they should quickly get debt free, so that they are free to serve God. Further development of the business will mostly be done out of retained profits.

Massive debt is not essential for trade and economic growth. An economy can grow without big increases in debt if businesses rely on shareholder equity for expansion. Those that are growing really fast might need to take on extra shareholders. If they need a loan to expand, they will need to obtain it from people that trust them. However, debt and loans will be much less important than it is in the modern economy and equity finance more common.

If they are obeying God, followers of Jesus should be in a position where they will not need to borrow.

> You will lend to many nations but will borrow from none. The Lord will make you the head, not the tail. If you pay attention to the commands of the Lord your God that I give you this day and carefully follow them, you will always be at the top, never at the bottom (Deut 28:12-13).

If God is with us, we should not need to go into debt. We will not be at the bottom of the heap, so we should not need to borrow.

Apart from productive debt, God's people should try to avoid debt. They should avoid borrowing to buy consumption goods. God wants his people to be free to obey him. If they are in debt, they do not have that freedom (Prov 22:7).

Banks are the Problem

Modern banks shift resources from productive to unproductive lending (in the hope of capital gains). The debt industry fails to distinguish between productive and unproductive investment. It treats them both as equally valuable, when clearly they are not.

According to the economic textbooks, banks act as intermediaries between savers and borrowers. Households deposit their surplus income in banks. In theory, the banks pool the deposits of savers and lend them to businesses to invest in plant and equipment that will make them more productive. Economists assume that banks assess the various opportunities and channel savings into the most effective investment options.

Modern banks rarely channel savings into productive equipment but feed them into increased prices for existing assets (mostly property). A large share of long-term lending by banks is for residential mortgages.

Banks prefer this type of lending because mortgages on dwellings are the best form of security. If the borrower defaults, the bank can foreclose on the mortgage and sell the dwelling to recover the money loaned, along with any penalty interest. Residential mortgage lending is an easy business for banks. It can only go wrong if dwelling prices plummet, making the house worth less than the amount owed to the bank.

Banks also make long-term loans to businesses. However, this is usually lending on mortgages for commercial real estate. Banks like this type of lending to businesses because the security is good. If the borrower defaults, they can foreclose and sell the property. This type of lending can only go wrong if commercial property prices collapse.

The problem with these types of lending is that they feed inflation of property prices. Banks have an endless capacity to make loans, provided they can find people with security who are willing to borrow. Their credit creation pushes up the price of property. Property buyers become heavily leveraged, which improves their returns from capital gains but leaves them vulnerable to an economic downturn.

In recent years, households and businesses have poured enormous resources and borrowed funds into property speculation. Their primary driver is hope for capital gains that are unrighteous wealth. Expansionary bank lending allows them to bid up prices, which has made their desire for capital gains self-fulfilling. These capital gains seem to justify further speculation in property.

Property price inflation penalises people dependent on wages and salaries and pensions. Debtors are subsidised at the expense of those on fixed incomes.

Apart from mortgage lending, most bank lending is short-term. Banks also provide short-term overdrafts to businesses to help them manage their operations. However, security, not economic development, is the main priority. The business is usually expected to provide collateral and the funding is quickly withdrawn if there are signs it is struggling.

Banks sometimes have subsidiaries providing hire purchase for transport equipment and plant and machinery. Hire purchase agreements provide the bank with security as ownership is not transferred until the debt is paid.

The debt industry rarely lends to a new business trying to get started or an existing business wanting to expand. They stick to safe investments with strong security. When a person wants to start a business, they usually need to mortgage their home to get the funds needed. The other option is to borrow from family and friends. Banks will usually not lend until the profitability of the new business is well established.

Banks get their profit from interest on outstanding debt, so they have a strong incentive to issue as much credit as possible, and the best way to do that is to fund speculative investments. The resulting price boom encourages people to take on more debt. Unfortunately, the cost of servicing this debt often grows faster than the income it produces, so it eventually drags on the economy, as debt costs become a growing share of income.

Creating Debt

Banks are key players in the debt industry, because they can create credit (see chapter 16). They have used this power to expand the massive burden of debt carried by households and businesses. Before the Kingdom of God comes to fullness, this burden will be swept away. The Jesus Jubilee will destroy the debt mountain and set people free.

Banks will be replaced by loan-organisers (see chapter 18). Instead of feeding property speculation, they will lend to businesses to help them develop and grow. They will focus on businesses that provide good employment and produce goods and services that people need. Loan-organisers will distinguish between unproductive and productive debt. They will avoid the former and encourage the latter. They will ensure that people are not burdened with unnecessary debt.

Cancellation of Debt

The modern world is weighed down by debt. The debt industry sits over the economy and sucks the life out of it. Governments support the debt industry by enforcing the repayment of debt. When human governments collapse, the debt industry will lose the ability to recover debts.

As the gospel advances, many debts will be cancelled as lenders come to realise that the income earned from lending to the poor is unrighteous wealth. Jesus' jubilee will bring a flood of debt cancellation for poor people.

Jesus varied his teaching on how to pray according to his audience. We prefer Luke's version because it speaks about forgiving sins (Luke 11:4). Matthew's version contains a starker message (which is mostly ignored).

Give us today our daily bread.
And forgive our debts,
  as we also have forgiven our debtors (Matt 6:12).

Everyone needs their food for the day, but Jesus links it to forgiving debts. People desperate for food need their debts forgiven. We assume that cancelling debts is a reference to forgiving sins, but if that were what he meant, Jesus would have used the word "hamartia" (as he did in Luke's version).

The Holy Spirit had a reason for prompting Matthew to record the version of the prayer where Jesus spoke about cancelling debts. The context was the Sermon on the Mount. Jesus had described what would happen when the Holy Spirit turned the world upside down. The poor will be raised up and the powerful brought down. People who have lent to the poor will give up expecting repayment.

Before speaking about prayer, Jesus spoke about giving to the poor. Afterwards, he spoke about treasures in heaven and warned about the danger of loving money. It was natural that in between, he would speak about debt because it was making poor people desperate. And much of the wealth of those who loved money was debt. Jesus' prayer reflected this situation.

The poor needed their debts cancelled, but this could only happen if creditors agreed to do it. The poor cannot force their creditors to cancel their debt. They must not use the government to make them do it. The most that they can do is pray that their debts will be cancelled and then leave the Holy Spirit to convict their creditors.

Everyone on earth owes God an enormous debt. People who have had their debt to him cancelled should look for ways to cancel the debts that other people owe to them. The gospel should result in a massive cancellation of debt, especially for the poor.

9

Land

A common form of unrighteous wealth is land acquired contrary to the Instructions for Economic Life. The only remedy for unrighteous land is to give it away.

Even Distribution

When Israel entered the Canaan, Joshua divided the land evenly between tribes and family groupings by casting lots (Joshua 15-19). God wants land evenly distributed everywhere. Land shared equally among the families of a community is righteous wealth. When a few powerful families or businesses hold all the land in a region, it has become unrighteous wealth.

In an agricultural society, land was the main form of productive asset. Distributing the land evenly ensured that every family had an equal economic opportunity. The land could be sold if the family got into financial difficulty, but God specified that they could get back any land they had lost at the next jubilee.

> In this Year of Jubilee everyone is to return to their own
> property (Lev 25:13).

This law ensured that each new generation got a fresh start.

Land Belongs to God

According to the Instructions for Economic Life, all land belongs to God. He created it, so he owns it. God allows us to use the land to build houses and grow crops. He gives us the produce of the land to use (he asked for the first fruits of the land to remind us that it is a gift from him (Ex 23:19)). However, the land itself belongs to God. Regardless of our title or ownership deed, all land is his property. The laws of nations cannot change this fact.

We can use the land, but we never own it. We are stewards of the land, so we must apply God's Instructions for Economic Life to its use.

Since God owns the land, any increase in the value of the land belongs to him. We can take produce off the land, but we cannot claim any capital gains for ourselves. People who make a capital gain by holding and selling land are stealing from God. Capital gain from selling land is unrighteous wealth that must be handed back to God by giving it away.

The Instructions for Economic Life made capital gains impossible. Land was held by families and passed from generation to generation. If a person fell into poverty, they could only sell the harvests until the next jubilee when the land had to be returned to the original family. The jubilee process limited the sale of land, so making capital gains was impossible. There was no market price for land because it belonged to God and could not be sold.

What is really being sold to you is the number of crops (Lev 25:16). The sale price was the value of crops that could be produced during the years between the sale and the next jubilee. This requirement prevented people from buying land to obtain capital gains.

Modern Solutions

The Instructions for Economic Life about land can be applied in the modern world without state coercion. The following principles are important.

- God owns the land
  The land belongs to God. This is true regardless of what our title or ownership deed says. When we buy and sell land, we can only sell the right to use it, not the land itself.

- Land should be evenly distributed
  We cannot start afresh, as the Israelites did when they entered the promised land. We must begin with the existing distribution and take voluntary actions to make it more even.

Land

- Voluntary giving and sharing
  People with plenty of land should give or share their land with those who have none.

- No debt
  Loans should be limited to a seven-year term. Re-payment of loans will be voluntary (see chapter 8). Land must not be loaded down with debt, as it is today. Land that belongs to God cannot be mortgaged, so most land will be free of debt. We can only borrow against future crops.

- No enforcement
  When the Kingdom of God has come, there will be no government to enforce the collection of debts, so banks will be reluctant to lend to buyers of land. Mortgage lending will shrink dramatically.

- No large holdings
  Large holdings of land will usually be unrighteous wealth because they were obtained by debt-leverage and inflation or by collusion with political powers.

- Avoid capital gains
  People owning land will avoid actions that would earn them capital gains that belong to God.

- No land banking
  Followers of Jesus should not engage in land banking because it earns unrighteous wealth.

- Every family
  God wants every family to have land on which to build a house and grow food. The food-growing land does not have to be in the same place as their home.

- No land rents
  Holding land and renting it to tenant farmers will often produce unrighteous wealth.

- Give away unrighteous wealth
  The only way to redeem unrighteous wealth is to give it away. Land that is unrighteous wealth should be given away. Capital gains belong to God, so they must be given away too.

These principles are not a justification for government enforced land redistribution, as that would just create more unrighteous wealth. All action regarding land must be voluntary. Owners should act when the Holy Spirit convicts them that their land is unrighteous wealth. They are free to decide what to do. Elders must not pressure believers to give away unrighteous wealth.

Once the gospel is successful and a significant proportion of the population has chosen to follow Jesus, their behaviour will affect everyone. It will become difficult to sell land for a high price if followers of Jesus are giving it away free. The price that people can get will fall dramatically and capital gains will disappear.

1. Agriculture Land

Developing Countries
In developing countries, access to land is really important. People without land have a very tough life, as they cannot grow food. Often the land is held by a few powerful landlords who rent small plots out to tenant farmers. This is unrighteous wealth. When these landlords come to faith in Jesus, they will realise their land is unrighteous wealth and choose to give some of their land away. This can be done in various ways.

- The land could be subdivided and given to the tenant farmers and other people who have no land. The cost of subdividing the land might be prohibitive in some legal environments.
- The landlord could hand the land over to the deacons in their church. They would set up a trust to hold the land and allow the farmers to rent it for a small fee that covers administration costs. The trustees would ensure that every-one who needs land got some. Because they would not need to pay exorbitant rent, farmers would need less land to make a living. Plots could be smaller and more widely distributed.
- The landowner could continue to hold the land as a trust from God. They would lease the land rent-free to people who need land, in the same way as the deacons above. This would be a risky option, as the person holding the land would

be open to the spirit of greed attached to the land. They could be tempted to take money for themselves.

- The deacons might organise the existing tenants into a cooperative that holds the title to the land on their behalf. The establishment deed of the cooperative would need some important conditions.
    - People should only have as much land as they need.
    - Land should be allocated to as many people as possible, not just to existing tenants.
    - The land should not be sold. Cooperative members would have a right to use the land, but not sell it.
    - The cooperative members will pay administration costs.

Land that is unrighteous wealth should be allocated in a way that will advance the Kingdom of God by encouraging followers of Jesus to establish Kingdom Communities. Some land would be used to produce food for other communities in nearby cities.

In a tribal society, the land is often controlled by a chief or elders on behalf of the tribe. This is fine, provided that they ensure that the land is allocated fairly and that everyone who wants to use the land gets a share.

If the chief or the elders give extra shares of land to their friends or families, or keep the best land for themselves, they are breaching their trust and slipping into unrighteous wealth. These unrighteous gains should be given away.

Foreign-Owned Lands

In some developing countries, much of the agricultural land is owned by foreign corporations. They rent the land to people who grow the crops for the corporation to export. Food becomes scarce and most people become dependent on expensive imported food.

In the Kingdom of God, there will be no government to protect the interests of foreign owners of land. When people come to faith, their elders might decide that the foreign-owned land is unrighteous wealth. They might tell their people that they do not need to pay rent to the foreigners. The elders might set up a trust or cooperative to hold the land instead. They would ensure that the use of the land was distributed evenly to everyone who needed it.

Ideally, the shareholders of the foreign corporation would come to faith and realise that they hold unrighteous wealth. If they decided to give the land away to people who are poor, it would be a huge blessing to the people in the developing country.

Developed Countries
In the developed world, most people live in cities and are not interested in farming. In this situation, land that is unrighteous wealth should be given to people who want work in farming.

Agricultural land should mostly be owned by the people who farm it. Land owned by absentee owners is usually unrighteous wealth. After years of collusion with governments, many of the following categories of farm will be unrighteous wealth.

- Farms that have been paid for by debt-leverage and inflation.
- Land holdings bigger than needed to support a family.
- Land received in return for loyalty to a political leader.
- Large company-owned farms where the shareholders do not work on the land.
- Land seized by creditors after owners defaulted on their debt.
- Land purchased with unrighteous wealth.
- Land seized during a military invasion.
- Land stolen by deception or fraud.
- Farms purchased by stealth through government collusion.

God will show those who seek him if their land is unrighteous wealth. Those who are convicted of owning unrighteous wealth will need to give it away. Often only a part of the land will be unrighteous wealth. In this case, the owner might only need to give away some of their land. The Holy Spirit will show them how much and how they should go about it.

The person holding the unrighteous wealth could deal with the land themselves, or they could let the deacons in their church handle it on their behalf.

- They could get people who want to be involved in farming to join them in a share-farming scheme and work for a percentage of the profit the farm earns.

- The farm could be subdivided into small units and leased or sold to people who want land for agricultural use. Land is most productive when worked by families who have an interest in it.
- If only part of the farm is unrighteous wealth, the owner might decide to make part of his land available to other people willing to use it and care for it.
- A trust could be established to hold the land and allocate it to people wanting to work in agriculture. The land belongs to God, so it would be the use of the land that is allocated.

The trust holding the land that has been given away might change the use of the land from capital-intensive farming to a more labour-intensive approach so that more people can be employed.

The land should generally be allocated in a way that would strengthen the local Kingdom Community. Christians giving away land would ensure that there are enough followers of Jesus among those taking up the land to form a new neighbourhood church. In some areas, the people owning the land could build homes in a central place so that they can form a new Kingdom Community.

If enough farmers give up their unrighteous wealth in land, there should be sufficient farmland available for everyone who wants to work in agriculture.

In difficult economic times, people may need to move from the city to the country where they can grow food. Groups of Christians could come together to support each other and grow food for each other and to supply other communities. People experienced in growing food could teach others how to do it.

God wants land used for producing food, not making money. As the gospel advances and more and more unrighteous wealth is given away, agriculture will change significantly. More people will work in agriculture and land will be more evenly distributed. Farms will focus on growing food as efficiently as possible.

2. Residential Land

Two principles are really important for residential land.

- Land must not be encumbered with debt because God is the owner and lending to people to buy land will be limited.
- Owning more than one house can be unrighteous wealth.

When the gospel advances in a city, large numbers of people will have unrighteous wealth to deal with. The two main types are:

- Houses owned but not lived in can be unrighteous wealth.
- Houses purchased with debt-leverage and inflation can be unrighteous wealth.

Many new followers of Jesus will have to give away a house that they own.

When giving away unrighteous wealth, followers of Jesus should do it in a way that advances the Kingdom of God. Jesus said,

> I say to you, make friends for yourselves by means of the unrighteous wealth (Luke 16:9).

Unrighteous wealth should be used to strengthen Kingdom Communities.

- Some new believers will sell their spare home and buy a second home in the area where a Kingdom Community is based. They could make it available to people who are committed to the Kingdom Community. This would help other followers of Jesus to move into the neighbourhood.
- Some followers of Jesus might sell a house and buy another in an area where apostles are planning to start a new neighbourhood church. The house could be made available for one of the apostles to live in when they are ready to begin.
- Others might use the sale proceeds to buy a house for some of the poorer people living in their Kingdom Community. Life would be easier for them if they did not have to pay rent.
- Some followers of Jesus might sell the spare house and use the money to start a business within their Kingdom Community to provide work for people needing employment.
- Others might give a house to a needy family who has no home in which to live.
- If the house is owned with a large mortgage, it might need to be sold to pay off the debt.

Several different solutions could be used.

- The owner might give the home to the deacons to handle. They could place the house in a trust that specifies how it has to be used (rent would be limited to maintenance costs).
- The owner might retain legal ownership of the house but give up the right to use it. This is risky, as the owner might fall into the temptation to use it for their own benefit.
- Another option might be for the owner to retain the legal title but give the deacons in the neighbourhood church responsibility for tenanting the house.
- If only part of the house is unrighteous wealth, the owner might need to sell it and buy one that is worth less, so they can extract the unrighteous wealth to give away.

The legal arrangement does not matter too much, as long as everyone understands that the land belongs to the Lord and unrighteous wealth is given away. People giving away unrighteous wealth will support people committed to a Kingdom Community.

In large cities, many people live in high-rise apartments. In these situations, the land is often owned by a body corporate, but the same principle applies as with other residential dwellings. People should usually own only one home. Those who have more than one might need to give an apartment away if it is unrighteous wealth. If the gospel advances and these principles are applied, the price of apartments should drop significantly.

Growing Food
People living in cities will need the opportunity to grow food for themselves. The leaders of a Kingdom Community will try to ensure that every family has access to land to grow some food

When people with unrighteous wealth are giving away bare land in the city or on the edge of the city, they should sometimes make it available for people who want to grow food. This could be done in different ways.

- The owner of the land might establish a community garden and allow anyone who wants to grow food to use it.
- The land might be split into small allotments that can be used by people who want their own small garden.

- Sometimes land might be given to a group of people who want to grow food to give away to people in need.

Rural-Urban Boundaries

The boundary of most cities gradually expands. Land on the edge of a city or town increases in value because it is sub-dividable into residential lots. The people owning this land often make a large capital gain when they sell it to developers. This land belongs to God, so taking a capital gain would be unrighteous wealth. Nothing has been done to earn it.

If followers of Jesus own sub-dividable land, they should choose to avoid capital gains that would be unrighteous wealth. They could give some of the land away and still hold land of equivalent value to what they had before. This would save them from taking unrighteous wealth for themselves.

They might give the land to developers working for the Kingdom of God, who would subdivide it into residential lots. These could be sold at a price sufficient to cover the cost of the infrastructure, including roading, lighting, electricity, sewerage and drainage. These residential lots will be much cheaper than usual because the capital gains of land bankers and speculators will not be built into the price. If enough followers of Jesus took this approach, the price of residential lots should dramatically decline.

The aim will be to use the new sub-divisions to advance the Kingdom. A proportion of the new residential lots will be sold to followers of Jesus. This would ensure that the new subdivision would have a neighbourhood church. Some apostles might move in to start the process.

If the landowners thought that the businesses undertaking the development would just take all the capital gain, they could sell the property to developers for the full market price and give the surplus into the Kingdom of God. Either option would be appropriate, provided they ensured that the capital gains that belong to God go to him, not into their own pockets.

The same approach will apply to situations where land is needed for new factories, roading or other infrastructure processes.

Followers of Jesus will want to avoid capital gains that would become unrighteous wealth.

Intergenerational Transfers

If large mortgages are not possible, because lending is limited to seven years, and repayment of debt is voluntary, young people will need more help from their families and their Kingdom Community to buy a home.

The children of Israel had inheritance rules, under which the family property passed to the oldest child. The inheriting child was expected to look after their parents in old age and support other members of their family. This process for transferring productive assets from one generation to the next has been broken by heavy taxation and mortgage debt.

Young people now take out loans to pay for their education. They get deeply into debt at a very young age. They get further indebted when they purchase a house. Having very little real savings, they have to purchase their house with a mortgage that is often ninety to a hundred percent of the value of the house. This worked well for most of the last half-century while governments were inflating their currencies and property prices rose relentlessly. With the mortgage fixed in nominal dollars and prices rising rapidly, the debt was wiped out by time.

At the same time, older people are expected to save for their retirement. Once their children have left home and their education and housing debts had been shrunk by inflation, they have to push money into the debt industry to build up funds to support themselves in retirement. This is difficult because inflation fights against them. They receive interest on their savings, but it is quickly eroded away.

Although these processes take place independently, the debt industry combines them into a massive wealth-shifting machine. Young people need money to pay for their education and homes. The banking system lends them what they need. Older people saving money for retirement hold their savings in the debt industry.

The debt industry becomes a machine that takes the savings of the parent's generation and recycles it to their children. Inflation assists the process by wiping out the debts of the indebted younger generation while eating away at the wealth of their parents.

Paying the debt industry to make the transfer is costly and robs everyone, except those inside the system. The financiers make money at both ends of the pipe. While young people are waiting for inflation to wipe away their debt, they pay a huge amount of interest, often more than the value of their house. The parents want high interest and low risk, so they save their money in the banks that fund house mortgages, or mortgage-backed securities. They often get an interest rate that is less than the inflation rate, so they are paying at their end of the pipe too.

The big beneficiary of this flow from one generation to the next is the debt industry. It charges fees at every point on the pipe, and those on the inside grab huge salaries and bonuses.

The global financial crisis in 2007 showed that this pipe is broken. At the parent's end of the pipe, money saved for the future suddenly disappeared into a black hole of risk. People who thought their future was secure, suddenly found that it was scary. At the other end of the pipe, house prices that were supposed to rise forever plummeted. Mortgages that were supposed to be shrinking ended up worth more than the house.

We need a better process for transferring wealth from one generation to the next. Paying the banking system to make the transfer is costly and robs everyone, except those inside the system.

This debt system creates deeper attitudinal problems. Young people learn to live with high levels of debt at a very young age. They are encouraged into property speculation as the best way to build up assets. This creates bad attitudes to work, debt and risk. Wealth comes from speculation, not by hard work and thrift.

The older generation is encouraged to live for the short-term. If they can put together some short-term savings to keep themselves going for a few more years, they can consume everything they earn. They have no incentive to build a long-term inheritance.

Inheritance

God is concerned about families and households.

> I am the God of your father, the God of Abraham, the God
> of Isaac and the God of Jacob (Ex 3:6).

God is not saying that he likes these three men. Rather, he saw them creating a spiritual and material inheritance to be passed on from one generation to the next. Jacob should have built on what Isaac had established. Isaac inherited spiritual gifts, wisdom and wealth from his father Abraham. This is not each generation looking out for itself. Rather, each generation built on what the previous generation has done to do greater things for God.

We must think the same way. Instead of children building their own wealth through speculation and leverage, they should be guarding and building their family inheritance. Instead of parents caring for themselves and consuming the rest, they should be building a spiritual and material inheritance that their family can build on in the future.

God's people should develop ways to make an inter-generational transfer that bypasses the debt industry so that bankers cannot clip the ticket at every step of the way. The transfer of spiritual capital is most important. The material transfer should follow the transfer of spiritual capital so that the Kingdom of God is built and God is glorified.

Instead of saving within the debt industry, parents will invest in their children's education. Some will start a business that some of their children can work in. When their children are leaving home, the parents will buy a smaller house so they can use the surplus to help their children get a place to live. At the other end, children will need to care for the parents in old age, rather than placing them in rest homes that will strip all their assets. That way they will continue being helpful in the family business.

God's people should aim to build a family inheritance. That inheritance might include a business, some homes, and perhaps a ministry. Building an inheritance should be an important objective for every family. Achieving this goal will be much easier if the family lives within a Kingdom Community.

Change Society

The advance of the gospel will bring a big change in the distribution of land. In a secular society, land tends to become more and more unequally distributed. Rich people tend to buy up more land to preserve their wealth, and poor people often have to sell their land in order to live. In the extreme, a few rich landlords end up owning much of the land.

In a society where the Kingdom of God is advancing, the opposite will happen. People with large holdings will be convicted about their unrighteous wealth when they hear the gospel. They will give some of their land to people who have none. The result will be fewer people with large holdings of land and houses. More people will have land to use and a home to live in.

Land should be shared evenly within a Kingdom Community. Parents will share their land with their children. People with large land holdings will give some of their land to those who have none (Barnabas is an example). Some will give the land while others may just share the land by allowing others to use it. People with large land holdings will give some of their land to communities that are squeezed for space.

Of course, there will be exceptions. Some people will reject the gospel and continue to own large holdings of land or multiple houses. Other people will continue to mess up their lives and become poor. However, as the gospel advances, these will become the exception rather than the rule. Fewer people will hold large blocks of land, and fewer people will be poor. The trend will be towards a more even distribution of the land.

10
Buying and Selling

Trade

No one has the skills needed to produce everything that they need, so an efficient economy needs a way for people to obtain goods and services that have been produced by others. There are only five ways that a person can get something that has been produced by someone else.

- **Theft** - People can get things they have not produced by stealing, but the Bible forbids theft.
- **Force** - People who are bigger and tougher can force someone else to hand over the goods or services they have produced. Using force to obtain stuff from other people is not permitted in God's economy.
- **Love** - People will give things that they produce to people they love. Love is very generous, but it does not stretch very far. It is effective in families and Kingdom Communities.
- **Compassion** - People motivated by compassion will give things to those in need. Compassion reaches further than love but is less generous. Followers of Jesus will show compassion when they meet people in need.
- **Buying and Selling** – A market is a space that allows people to sell things they do not want and buy things that they need. It enables them to specialise in producing what they are good

at doing and buy what they need from others. In the world, most transactions will be by buying and selling.

Specialisation and Efficiency

Specialisation is good, as it began with the Trinity. Each person of the Trinity took on a specialised task for the benefit of all. Specialisation brings big economic benefits to the world.

Economic development occurs when people specialise in producing what they are good at doing. They sell their surplus and use what they earn to buy what they need from others who have specialised in producing other things.

Specialisation generally increases efficiency. When a person can concentrate on a set of tasks, they can learn to do them effectively. The people who designed my computer produced an efficient product. If there were no markets and no specialisation, they would have to spend their days cultivating food crops or hunting game. They would be worse off, and I would be worse off too because I could not make a computer in a thousand years.

A person who chooses to specialise and buy and sell comes under pressure to operate efficiently. They must offer the goods for sale at a price sufficient to cover their production costs but pushing their price too high will dramatically reduce their sales. They have to choose between higher prices and more sales. This dilemma forces an ambitious business to reduce the costs of production by finding ways to be more efficient. This allows them to increase their income, without raising prices and losing sales.

Markets Reduce Search Costs

Specialisation benefits everyone, but people can only specialise if there is a way for others to obtain what they have produced. Markets where goods and services can be offered for sale allow people to specialise in what they do best.

A market is a space where people can display or describe items offered for sale, and buyers can make offers to buy. It is primarily an information sharing place where people display the goods they are offering to sell, and others can state the price at which they are willing to buy.

Buying and Selling

Markets can be physical or virtual. An economy is made up of a great number of different markets, ranging from market stalls to shopping malls to online systems like eBay. Each of these is an information system that allows people to offer products for sale and others to make or accept offers for them.

Honest markets facilitate efficiency by reducing search costs. Bringing together people with surplus products reduces the costs of selling because buyers are easier to find. A market makes it easy for people who do not know each other to find someone who wants what they have to sell.

Markets allow wise people to display their innovations. The best innovations are rewarded with more customers.

Offers

A market is a place for displaying offers. They are the heart of a market. In an honest market, an "offer" has four elements.

- An offer describes goods or services being offered for sale.
- The offer describes the quality of the items being offered.
- The offer specifies the price the seller is willing to accept.
- The offer explains how and when the goods or services will be delivered to a person who accepts the offer.

An offer is quite benign. No one has to accept it. If everyone thinks it is a bad offer, it will just be ignored. There is nothing in the scriptures suggesting that making unrealistic offers is morally wrong, although it probably is wasted effort.

A transaction in an honest market consists of several parts.

- A potential seller makes an offer.
- A buyer accepts the offer.
- The buyer pays the seller the agreed price.
- The seller delivers the goods or services offered to the buyer.

An offer only becomes a sale when accepted by another person. Once a buyer has accepted the offer, it becomes a binding contract. The Bible condemns those who fail to complete contracts that they have freely entered. Failure to complete the contract is theft.

Benefits of Buying and Selling

In an honest market, the buyer and the seller both benefit from a transaction. A sale can only occur if two conditions are met.

- The seller must want the money being offered more than they want the thing they are selling.
- The buyer must want the thing being sold more than they want the money they are offering.

Both the buyer and the seller get what they wanted, so they are both better off after the transaction. The buyer has a good they wanted. The seller gets the money they need to buy what they want. In an honest market, sales only occur if both the buyer and the seller believe they will be better off.

No one is made worse off in an honest market. The only people disappointed are those unable to sell the items they hoped to sell. They were unable to find someone who valued the item higher than they did, but they still have what they came with, so they are not made worse off. Some potential buyers may be disappointed if they did not find what they want, but they still have the money they came with, so they are not worse off either.

A market is a place for information sharing. Anyone can buy or sell in an honest market provided:

- there is no deception in the offers;
- the seller owns the thing being offered;
- there is no coercion;
- and the buyer and seller freely agree on the price.

Market Morality

A market is not a moral entity that can be judged as right or wrong. A market cannot make decisions or take actions. It is simply a place for information sharing. Three groups of moral actors are involved in a market.

- The owners of the market set the rules under which the market operates. If their rules allow cheating or coercion, the owners are immoral.
- Sellers are responsible for their offers. Selling stolen goods or lying about the quality of what is being sold is morally wrong.

- Buyers are acting immorally if they pay for goods with counterfeit money, or if they use force to make someone sell at a lower price.

Claims that a market is evil are wrong. Markets are neither good or evil because they do not act or make decisions. Their character is determined by the words and actions of participants in a market.

Honest markets allow people to choose what they want to buy. They do not dictate what a person's choices should be. If people want a simple life, they are free to choose it and market participants will usually deliver it to them. If they want bad things, they will mostly find what they want.

Evil desires come from the human heart fed by false ideas twisted by spiritual powers. The best way to change choices is to proclaim the gospel in the power of the Spirit. If people are making bad choices, the church has failed in its calling to change hearts and assist them to grow in wisdom.

Regulating Markets

A market is a place where people can display their offers. Laws against theft already deal with problems that may arise.

- Preventing markets from forming helps the owners of existing markets, but not buyers or sellers.
- Limiting the types of offers that can be made is pointless because nobody is obliged to accept them.
- Controlling the price range that can be specified in offers seems to be pointless, as no one will agree to the prices offered if they are too high.
- Preventing certain types of people from accepting offers benefits other sellers, but not buyers.
- Preventing people from making offers that are deceptive or fraudulent is already covered by laws against theft.
- Failure to deliver products once a sale is agreed is dealt with by laws against theft.

Markets provide people with information about the offers being made. Once this is understood, most demands for regulation of markets do not make sense.

Price Information

Prices contain useful information about the value that assists businesses to decide about the viability of potential projects. These price signals help businesses allocate their resources to activities where they can be used most effectively.

A big problem for the Soviet Union was that with no real prices, it became impossible to allocate resources effectively. The result was that businesses produced too much of some things and not enough of others. This led to wastage and shortages that could only be solved by rationing.

Markets for business services, intermediate goods, and capital goods are essential. The prices agreed in these markets allow businesses to decide between a range of production possibilities.

Setting Prices

Markets do not set prices. Various people can specify a price at which they are willing to sell. Others may offer to buy at a different price. Some will not enter the market because the prices offered are outside the range that would interest them.

Prices are never really set in a market. A sale occurs when a buyer and seller agree on a price, but that does not set the price. A transaction at that price may never occur again. Buyers and sellers only set the price for their transaction. It might influence later transactions, but it does not set the price for them.

A business can set a price at which they will sell a product, but they cannot force people to buy at that price. If the price is too high, people will refuse to buy from that business. Another business could undercut them with a lower price. A standard price can only be established if sellers collude to set it. When that happens, the market is not honest but has been corrupted.

I don't like the term "free market" as most markets are not free at all. They are usually controlled by government regulations or dominated by a few large corporations. Freedom is often taken as a right to be selfish and dishonest. I prefer the term "honest market". When buyers and sellers comply with God's Instructions for Economic Life, they establish an honest market.

Instructions for Economic Life

God allows buying and selling in markets, but his Instructions for Economic Life place significant restraints on buyers and sellers. Followers of Jesus must apply these principles whenever they enter a market to buy and sell. Honesty is the main requirement.

> Differing weights and differing measures—the Lord detests them both (Prov 20:10).

> The Lord detests differing weights, and dishonest scales do not please him (Prov 20:23).

In Biblical times, a merchant would supply the scales used for buying and selling. When buying something they would use heavy weights and when selling they would use the light scales. Using different weights, they could steal from people without them even knowing they had been robbed. God detests this practice.

This instruction applies to all types of dishonesty with buying and selling. God's people must be honest about the quality of what they are selling. They must give an honest description without exaggerating features or covering up defects. God dislikes advertising that gives false information about a product. Seductive methods of advertising that play to people's weaknesses and insecurities have no place amongst God's people.

The seller has an advantage in most transactions because they understand the quality of what they are selling better than the buyer (economists call this asymmetric information). A seller must not use this advantage to deceive a buyer. The seller must ensure that their neighbour understands the quality of what they are buying.

God's people must not take advantage of people who are poor when buying and selling.

> Do not take advantage of each other, but fear your God. I am the Lord your God (Lev 25:17).

Poor people enter a market under tremendous pressure because they need to sell something to buy what they need. If a buyer knows this, they could offer a very low price and the seller would have to take it, because they are desperate. If a person selling recognises the plight of someone who is hungry, they could charge a high price, and the frantic person would have to pay it or starve. This kind of behaviour is forbidden in the Instructions for Economic Life.

Whoever is kind to the needy honours God (Prov 14:31).

Whoever is kind to the poor lends to the Lord, and he will reward them for what they have done (Prov 19:17).

Followers of Jesus must be generous to the poor when they are buying and selling. We must not take advantage of people who are desperate to buy or sell. Price gouging during a crisis is wrong.

He who withholds grain, the people will curse him,

But blessing will be on the head of him who sells it (Prov 11:26).

During a famine, when people are desperate for food, people with food to sell can be tempted to hoard it and make a big profit when the price has soared. A rising price is useful for rationing the supply of a good that is scarce, but once it goes above a certain level, it becomes an unfair burden on the community. Hoarding scarce goods during a crisis for an excessive price is wrong (James 5:3). Income gained in this way is unrighteous wealth.

God did not give governments authority to enforce the Instructions for Economic Life. He prefers that people do what is right because they love him or are convicted by the Holy Spirit.

Generous Buying and Selling

Jesus defined our neighbour as anyone we meet during daily life (Luke 10:36-37). The people we meet when buying and selling in a market are neighbours, so we have a responsibility to treat them with kindness and respect.

When selling, we should not always go to the highest bidder. We might decide to sell to the person with the greatest need, at a price that they can afford. When dealing with people facing poverty, we could invite the buyer to specify the price that they can afford to pay. Allowing poor people to pay what they can afford is an effective way of helping them.

You must not sell them food at a profit (Lev 25:37).

When buying, we might decide to buy from a person who is poor and offer to pay a higher price than other people are willing to pay. Followers of Jesus who have prospered could bless the seller by paying a price that reflects what the product is worth to them. If some people are generous in this way, the seller will be able to allow poorer people a lower price.

Followers of Jesus will be generous when buying and selling, even if they are sometimes ripped off by people of the world. They will look for ways to bless other people rather than seeking deals that benefit themselves.

As the gospel advances, the balance will shift from buying and selling to loving and sharing. Strengthening communities giving and sharing will be more important for them than making a profit.

Adding Value

Profit is a crude measure of the extent to which the business has made people better off. The cost of production reflects the value of the components, materials and labour used in production. The price received roughly reflects the value to buyers purchasing the product. The difference between sales and costs indicates the additional value created by the producer.

Profit = income - expenditure

Profit ≈ value added

This is new value that did not exist before. The producer created value by making the product and by finding people who want it.

To make a profit, a business must add value. They must take raw materials and components and put them together in a way that makes them more useful to other people. The components must be worth more when put together in the product than they were worth separately. That is adding value.

When producers add value, they tend to make a profit. This means profit is good. The scriptures confirm it.

> All hard work brings a profit, but mere talk leads only to poverty (Prov 14:23).

> The plans of the diligent lead to profit as surely as haste leads to poverty (Prov 21:5).

Businesses make money by adding value. To make a profit, they must have produced goods or services that made people better off.

To succeed in an honest market, businesses must serve their consumers. Honest markets allow consumers to follow their preferences, but they are constraining for businesses. A business that does not provide what their customers want will struggle.

Government

Governments do something different. Most of the services they provide are free, so they do not have to add value to ensure that people want them. We assume it is good that governments do not make profits, but this makes them dangerous. People do not have to pay, so the government does not have to provide services that make them better off.

Governments function by taking from one person and giving it to another. This is a zero-sum situation. Governments can only help one person by taking from another. They do not add value but shift value from one person to another. The process of taking from one and giving to another has a cost.

Economic Providence

Many people expect free markets to act as economic providence. They believe that free markets can "work all things together for good". Anyone understanding markets knows that this is not true. Markets are not rational entities, so they cannot act to produce a perfect world. Only God works all things for good (Rom 8:28).

The belief that free markets work everything for good is totally unrealistic. Foolish transactions can make people worse off. Dishonest markets have allowed terrible evils to occur. Those who equate markets with providence trust in a false religion.

In an honest market, people governed by the Instructions for Economic Life, people are less likely to be harmed by buying and selling, but wise guidelines cannot prevent people from making unwise purchases or sales. Everything does not work for good, for those who reject God, even if they make smart economic decisions.

11

Business

Business is a great vehicle for human creativity. Being made in the image of God, humans have amazing creative ability. Businesses produce a wonderful array of products and services with the potential to improve human life in many ways. Competition for customers encourages businesses to develop new technology and find more efficient ways to make products and provide services.

Good and Evil
Business has been blamed for much of the evil in the world, but this is only partly true. Businesses have done evil things, but they have also been the source of much that is good.

A business is just a group of people organised to work together for an agreed purpose. The nature of the business will be determined by the character of those people and the customers of the business. If the people in control are good, the business should be a force for good. If the people in control are not pursuing good, then it could be a force for evil. The activities of a business will reflect the character of its owners and managers.

Businesses rely on customers. To succeed, a business must supply its customers with what they want. Customers will often want things that are not good, so supplying bad things will usually be profitable. If a business does not have good managers, they can be tempted into activities that advance evil.

Business can be a force for good or evil. This chapter highlights some ways that business has gone astray, sometimes by being too effective. The next chapter explains how businesses led by good have an important role in God's Economy.

Prosperity

The development of business has brought great amazing prosperity to the world. Until the Industrial Revolution, most people lived a subsistence lifestyle. In many places, earning enough to buy food and shelter was a struggle. Even people with trade skills were only a short step away from disaster. Life was often painful and short.

The industrial revolution allowed human initiative and inventiveness to flourish and set the western world on a path to much greater wealth. Steam power replaced horse and water power. Large factories using complicated machinery enabled the mass production of a wide range of goods. These changes eventually improved the lives of people living in cities.

The development of international trade gave businesses access to cheaper raw materials and opened up mass markets. Improved transport technologies allowed greater specialisation, which increased business productivity. The invention of the shipping container allowed businesses to transport goods from one side of the world to the other. Businesses seeking profits shifted production to the places where labour was cheapest. They bring components together from various places, assemble products and deliver them all over the world.

The global system of production that brought unprecedented wealth to the western world has now spread to Asia and many other parts of the world. In a couple of centuries, much of the world moved from a struggle to live to a life of comparative abundance.

Modern people can choose from a vast range of cheap goods and services that earlier generations only dreamt about. Economists assumed that if people became more prosperous, they would work less and enjoy more leisure. That has not happened. Instead, most people work as hard as ever because their needs seem to be greater. It seems that the more we have, the more we need. Abundance has become normal, but it often does not feel like it.

Feeding Selfishness

We can have too much of a good thing. The success of business has turned people into isolated consumers choosing between a limitless range of consumer goods and services. Individuals can meet their needs without depending on anyone else, which encourages selfishness.

The modern economy plays a trick. It has created abundance, but it also makes us feel like we do not have enough. We find ourselves working hard to buy a lot of stuff that we do not need.

- Deceptive advertising seduces us to want more and more.
- Creative businesses use clever marketing to create new desires by manipulating our insecurity and craving for status.
- Advertising campaigns encourage people to covet people who have more than they do.
- Advertisers are skilled at making people want things that they did not know they needed.
- Businesses are incredibly creative, so inventors are continually developing new ways for us to amuse ourselves.
- Marketers develop new gadgets and appliances and persuade us that we cannot live without them.
- Manufacturers constantly produce new models with better features that everyone should have.
- Brands and labels make ordinary goods like shoes expensive.
- Many products wear out after being used for a short time
- People work long hours to buy things that do not satisfy.

The inflated promises of modern business eventually end in disappointment when the goods we wanted fail to satisfy. The more we have, the less enjoyment things produce.

Resource Extraction

To feed the capital-intensive industrial production that supports our excessive consumption, businesses have extracted resources from the earth wherever they can be found. Businesses in the modern world assume that the resources that are there are available to be used by the current generation. If they discover new mineral resources, they have to be extracted and used as soon as possible.

No one suggests that resources be left for future generations. Most of the oil on the planet will be used within a few centuries by four or five generations. This would be fine if life on earth were certain to end soon. But if life on earth goes on for another two millennia, there may not be enough oil for all potential needs, because most of it was used up during a few selfish centuries.

Most oil has been used as fuel. Some is made into plastics, which are used briefly and then sent to the landfill. Waste plastic is cluttering up the oceans. This is short-sighted, as future generations might have more beneficial uses for oil. We should be thinking about the resources we are going to leave for future generations?

Part of the problem is that oil and mineral resources are controlled by governments that only think as far ahead as the next election. If we are committed to creating an inheritance for our great, great grandchildren and beyond, we would be thinking about what resources will be available for them.

God has not given the resources of the earth for the exclusive use of one or two generations. He has placed enough resources on the earth to last humans for its full history, but not enough to sustain generations of greed.

Collusion with Government

A serious problem in most modern economies is that many businesses collude with their government to obtain a privileged position. Many regulations protect incumbent businesses from competition. For example, businesses often ask the government to protect them from competition from imports. Business lobbyists always claim to be acting in the interest of the people, but the owners of the protected businesses usually benefit the most.

Collusion between business and government is always dangerous (Luke 3:14). When a business gains the support of the government, it can use the coercive powers of government to change what consumers buy. This may be good for the business, but consumers lose their freedom. Multinational businesses sometimes use their nation's military power to secure the resources they need. In the Kingdom of God, the political power will wither away, so this collusion with business will not be possible.

No Limited Liability

The worst collusion between government and business is limited liability laws. These laws limit the losses of shareholders in a failed company to the value of their original share contribution, even if their share of the company's debt is greater. These laws aim to encourage business growth by minimising the risk of losses.

Large corporations do not emerge naturally because the accumulation of risk would be too scary for anyone to contemplate. They were made possible when governments established limited liability laws to protect shareholders.

Limited liability laws have allowed corporations to operate on an enormous scale because individual shareholders are not accountable for all the corporation's debts or losses. Although these laws have fostered business, they transfer the risk of bad decisions from those responsible to innocent people. Limited liability allows company shareholders to make unlimited profits while limiting their losses if the company fails.

When governments pass limited liability laws, they are attempting to do something they do not have the power to do. Liability can only be removed when someone pays the price. Jesus was able to wipe out our liability for sin because he paid the penalty on the cross. Governments attempt to wipe out financial liability by simply decreeing that it will be limited. They do not have that power because they are unwilling to pay the price.

Government laws do not eliminate the liability for business losses; they just shift it to other people. When a limited liability company goes bust, the shareholders walk away with limited losses. The rest of the losses do not disappear. They are shifted to the creditors of the failed company. The sub-contractors, employees and customers who have traded with the business in good faith have to bear the cost.

Limited liability laws foster bad decision making by encouraging excessive risk-taking and short-term profit making. Businesses that take big risks earn large profits without worrying about the risks. Shareholders earn better dividends due to excessive risk-taking but limit their losses during the bad years that inevitably follow.

The common belief that businesses cannot develop and grow without limited liability laws is not true. Businesses will continue to grow, but they will have to be much more careful about the way they operate. Boards of directors will have to scrutinise the actions of their company management more carefully. Shareholders will have to keep a close eye on what the company directors are doing. Better stewardship should result.

Jesus warned his listeners to count the cost and assess the risks before making decisions (Luke 15:28-29). If investors know that they will carry the full costs of any failure, they will assess the risks and costs very carefully to make better business decisions.

Without limited liability laws, the directors of a business are still free to declare they will not cover liabilities beyond their initial contribution. If they included that in their articles of incorporation, it might be difficult to get a judgment against them for anything more if the business failed. However, they could have difficulty starting their business, because other businesses would not trust them. They might have to pay for everything up front.

Destroyed Communities

Limited liability laws have encouraged the globalisation of business. Manufacturers moved their plants to places in the world where labour is cheapest. They went to Asia first, and now most are operating in China. They will eventually move on, if they can find cheaper labour.

Globalisation has pushed business specialisation and the division of labour as far as they can go. Consumer goods from China are incredibly cheap, so the people of the West have been buying like crazy. However, the cost had been paid by the communities that are left behind. The globalisation of business has disrupted local communities. We have sacrificed our communities for cheap consumption.

- The globalised production system needs industrialisation and urbanisation, but they destroy traditional communities and interrupt family relationships.
- People are overwhelmed and isolated, without reliable personal networks to provide support in time of trouble.

- The customs that constrained behaviour in traditional communities are thrown off because they seem hypocritical and repressive to the modern world.
- Casting off social restraints give people immense social and personal freedom. People can live for themselves without any moral accountability to anyone.
- The drive for efficiency separates people into winners and losers. Some succeed, but many are forced into precarious employment with meagre pay and harsh working conditions.
- Strugglers are forced to look to the state for assistance, but they are faced by an impersonal, uncaring, rules-driven bureaucracy, which leaves them feeling powerless and resentful. They often relieve their frustration by lashing out with aggressive, abusive and undisciplined behaviour.
- Socially disruptive behaviour has to be constrained by standardised, impersonal laws enforced by human governments.
- Despite the promised freedom, the state is more and more involved in intimate personal affairs. Political solutions are needed for issues that were once solved locally.
- Although all people are free and equal, the successful people have gained control of the economy and politics.
- The successful people congregate in wealthy suburbs of prosperous cities. Their personal freedom leaves them no obligation to care for others, except from a distance, through donations to "caring organisations".
- The people with the capacity to organise social and communal support tend to follow the winners out. The strugglers are left behind in ghettos where they are swamped by the global economy without support networks.

The solution to these problems is the advance of the gospel and giving and sharing in Kingdom Communities.

More and More

Modern businesses are great at producing the things that people want. The problem is that if people want more than they need, businesses will produce it anyway. If people decide that they want less, businesses will persuade them that they want more.

Economic development has made it possible for us to consume more and more. That would be great if "things" were the goal of life, but they are not. Jesus told a parable to illustrate the futility of getting "bigger and better" to "enjoy life". The land of this rich man yielded an abundant crop (Luke 12:16). This was probably unrighteous wealth. The man must have controlled a large area of land as it produced enough to fill several barns. He decided he would store his wealth and take life easy.

> I will tear down my barns and build bigger ones, and there I will store my surplus grain. And I'll say to myself, "You have plenty of grain laid up for many years. Take life easy; eat, drink and party (Luke 12:18-19).

The twist in the parable was that the man would die that night. He seemed to have been successful but had actually wasted his life. He would lose everything that he had worked hard to get.

> This is how it will be with whoever stores up things for themselves but is not rich toward God (Luke 12:21).

The rich man hoarded wealth for himself but was spiritually poor.

"Take life easy and party" is not an option for God's people. Jesus made the meaning of the parable clear.

> Be on your guard against all kinds of greed; life does not consist of an abundance of possessions (Luke 12:15).

The Greek word for "greed" means "having more". We should be on guard against wanting more and more because it is dangerous.

Western culture has forgotten Jesus' command and focussed on having more and more, and modern business has provided it. Jesus warned that this is dangerous because wealth accumulated on earth means nothing when we get to the next life. On the other hand, those who are rich toward God take their wealth with them.

Followers of Jesus find peace by serving Jesus. We must be careful that greed does not distract us from serving him. Those who have taken on a spirit of greed might need to give away some of their possessions to break that spirit. As the gospel advances and more people choose to follow Jesus, they will realise that seeking more and more possessions robs them of spiritual riches.

12
Business and the Kingdom

Most people spend about a third of their lives at work, usually in a business of some kind. Since business is such an important part of life, followers of Jesus should understand how businesses will operate under the Government of God.

Business Authority

Business is a good place to expand the authority of the Kingdom. A business begins when some people with skills and spare assets gives authority over them to a business organisation. Pooling assets increases their effectiveness. Often a group of people who belong to the same Kingdom Community will pool their resources and combine their skills to establish a business.

Businesses have limited and temporary authority. Owners can sell their shares in the business at any time. A business cannot force people to buy the goods and services it has produced. It cannot force people to work for it. Employees submit to the authority of the business, but they can resign from their employment when they choose. If a business is wound up, the authority it exercised disappears.

Businesses operate under Free Authority, which is the best type of authority. They cannot force people to do things against their will. Only governments have that power. A business can only exercise Imposed Authority if it is empowered by a government.

Business is a powerful tool for achieving results. Even if Adam and Eve had not sinned, business activity would have been needed, as it is the best way to manage the people and resources needed to care for the earth. A large part of the work of caring for the world that God has given to his people will have to be done by businesses. Followers of Jesus who want to help restore the world should look for opportunities to get involved in business activities.

Business is a good model for organising groups of people to work together on a common task, so exercising authority in business is essential for bringing the Kingdom of God to earth.

- Businesses employ people with complementary skills and get them to specialise in tasks that they are good at doing. This makes them more productive than they would be if they worked on their own.
- Businesses provide their employees with productive equipment that makes their work more effective. They increase the productivity of their employees by supporting their efforts with good equipment and technology.

Business is an effective tool for organising people and using productive assets to advance the Kingdom of God. Even in a hostile culture, followers of Jesus will usually be free to operate businesses that produce things that people need.

Employment
A business needs good employees to achieve its objectives. In return, they are expected to care for their employees and help them to develop to their full potential. Employers will help their staff find work that utilises their skills and gives them fulfilment.

Some people will choose to be self-employed, but many others will be more productive if they are employed by a business that can utilise their skills. The catch is that employment is a master/servant relationship in which the employer has authority over their employees. Businesses that are led by followers of Jesus must not take advantage of this vulnerability.

While employees are at work, they have to obey the instructions of their employer. Their manager can make them do things they might not want to do. If the employer mistreats them, their only option is to leave, but that leaves them without a source of income. Some will put up with mistreatment, so their family does not suffer.

Employers have a master in heaven, so they must treat their employees with the same justice and impartiality as they receive from him (Eph 6:9). They must not threaten them or force them to do things that are offensive to them. (Col 4:1).

Employers decide the remuneration of their staff. The Bible does not specify particular wage rates for particular roles. This would be impossible because wages vary according to the type of work, the skills of the employee, and the availability of other workers. What is low in one situation might be high in another. There is no such thing as a just wage.

However, God's Instructions for Economic Life set some boundaries on employment contracts. Employees are not disconnected people. They become the employer's neighbours, so they must be loved and cared for. Most employees are dependent on their work for getting the income that their family needs to live. An employer who is a good neighbour will pay employees sufficient to live on. Where possible, they will support their employees through difficult times.

Jesus told employers that they should be considerate of their employees. In the parable of the Workers in the Vineyard, he explained that employees must be paid enough to cover the necessities of life (Matt 20:1-16). If the people of God put this principle into practice, the impact on poverty would be huge.

The prophets condemned employers who defraud their employees (Mal 3:5).

> You shall not oppress a hired servant who is poor and needy, whether one of your brethren or one of the aliens who is in your land within your gates (Deut 24:14).

The word "oppress" (ashaq) means "press upon, oppress, violate, defraud, get deceitfully, extort". Forcing an employee who is destitute and desperate to accept a low rate of pay is oppression. An employer is not free to pay what the market will bear. An employer must not take advantage of the vulnerability of a person who is desperate for work when negotiating their wages.

135

Kingdom Communities

The leaders of a Kingdom Community will encourage people who trust in God to pool their resources to establish businesses that support their community.

- Good businesses can strengthen a Kingdom Community by providing employment and producing goods or services for the people living within it.
- The elders of neighbourhood churches will support people who are serving God in business. They will provide training and support them with prayer.
- Elders of a Kingdom Community will encourage businesses to provide employment for people that share in it.
- Employers have a great deal of influence and authority. Under modern economic conditions, very few people are willing to take responsibility for employing others. This has resulted in a serious unemployment problem.
- Employers have authority over their staff. An employee who accepts the authority of a Christian businessperson while they are at work is under the Government of God.
- Apostolic businesses will release their best staff and send them out to start new businesses. They might even provide them with some productive equipment to get started. This is opposite to the world, which tries to bring the best back to the centre.
- Incorporating a business as a company gives it a life beyond the life of its owners and managers. This enables a longer-term perspective on business decisions.
- If God has called them to it, followers of Jesus should seek positions in the business world. However, they should learn how business relates to the Government of God and the authority of Jesus.
- Followers of Jesus should pray for their brothers and sisters who are managers in the business world. These people are often under more intense spiritual pressure than Christians in full-time ministry in the church, yet they usually receive far less prayer support.

- The spiritual power behind business roles must be broken. Evil spirits attach to positions of authority. Unless the previous manager was a follower of Jesus walking in righteousness, evil spirits may have attached themselves to the role. If these spirits are not forced out, the new manager will find the going tough.

Business Objectives

A business can be used for good or evil, depending on the character of the people who exercise authority in it. If they are worldly, the business can encourage consumerism and materialism. Worldly businesses often seek to make a profit at all costs and ignore the impact on people and the creation. They often seek to manipulate demand for their products by seductive advertising.

On the other hand, a business with godly managers can be a powerful vehicle for advancing the Kingdom of God. As they come under the influence of Jesus, their objectives will change.

- **Kingdom of God** – The primary objective of every business will be to advance the Government of God. This goal will take precedence over every other objective.

  If the chief executive and directors of a business choose to follow Jesus and their decisions are accepted by the shareholders, the entire business belongs to the Kingdom. If they make their decisions in accordance with Jesus' will, all the authority in the business is submitted to him.

- **Honour God** – Business people will demonstrate integrity. They will avoid actions or activities that dishonour God.

- **Bless people** – The owners and managers of a business will love their neighbours. They will focus on providing goods or services to people who need them. As more and more people choose to follow Jesus, people will lose interest in buying trivial goods. Businesses will not be able to manipulate people into buying things they do not need.

- **Bless employees** – Some business owners have abused their employees. In God's economy, they will treat them as neighbours. They will pay them enough to live on.

- **Efficient Use of Resources** – Businesses will use resources wisely. Scarce minerals will not be wasted but preserved for future generations.
- **Care for the Earth** – Businesses will avoid actions that are destructive of the earth. They will understand the travail of the earth under sin.

  > The whole creation has been groaning as in the pains of childbirth right up to the present time (Rom 8:22).

  Kingdom focussed businesses will participate in activities to liberate the creation from bondage to decay. They will help make the world a better place.
- **Protect the Weak** – In God's Economy, businesses will not take advantage of the weak. They will choose to lose profits rather than harm people.
- **Support the Gospel** – Profits earned from some Kingdom focussed businesses will be used to support the proclamation of the gospel.
- **Building Community** – Business leaders will understand the importance of local communities. They will avoid activities that would undermine the cohesion of these communities.
- **Long-term** – Long term goals will always be more important than short-term gains.
- **Righteousness** – Business leaders will do what is morally right, not just what is legally right.
- **Permanent Quality** – Planned obsolescence is common in modern economies. Most electronic goods and motor vehicles are designed with a limited life, so they need to be replaced every few years. This is good for business but bad for consumers. In the Kingdom Economy, businesses will develop products that will last for as long as they are needed.
- **Profit** – Businesses in the Kingdom Economy will need to make a profit so they can expand their investment in productive equipment. They will not seek exorbitant profit but will be satisfied with a reasonable return on their investment. Profits will not come ahead of other Kingdom objectives.

People living in Kingdom Communities will invest in businesses that utilise people's skills and use productive equipment to supply goods and services that others need.

After learning to operate their business within their Kingdom Community, groups of followers of Jesus could expand their activities into the wider business world. Businesses operated by the people of God will be welcome in a hostile world if they supply products that people need at an acceptable price.

Big Production Shift

Followers of Jesus should live a different life.

- Their primary goal will be sharing the gospel and building the body of Jesus.
- They will be more interested in helping the poor than getting more and more.
- They will be more concerned about strengthening relationships within their community than building wealth.
- They will value work less and time with people more.

Life in their community will change, so businesses will have to respond. Eventually, as more and more communities are transformed, the global economy will change too. The range of goods and services that businesses produce will shift dramatically as God's Economy grows.

- Businesses producing some consumption goods will face declining demand.
- Goods and services used by the poor will face rising demand.
- Seductive advertising will be less effective as people become secure in their status in Jesus. People will see through advertising that attempts to make them want things that they did not know they needed.
- Wants and desires will be inspired by the Holy Spirit rather than being manipulated by advertisers.
- People will stop coveting people who have more and seek to bless those who do not have as much as they do.
- Hearts that are full of the peace and joy of the Spirit will not need the latest devices and appliances to have a fulfilled life.

- People will not need to own the latest gadgets. They will get access to what they need through sharing with others.
- People will want reliable products, so manufacturers will need to design products with a longer life.
- The demand for financial services will decline. The debt industry will collapse and shrink.
- Nationalism will disappear, so war will become less prevalent. Defence will be managed at a local level. The large military equipment companies that dominate many modern economies will shrink and disappear. Some will have to switch to producing agricultural equipment to survive.

  > They will beat their swords into ploughshares
  > and their spears into pruning hooks.
  > Nations will not take up sword against nation,
  > nor will they train for war anymore (Mic 4:3).

- As society changes, local communities will be restored. Social life will return to local communities, so commuting for work or entertainment will decline. This will have a huge impact on the automobile industry. The demand for vehicles that are more useful within local communities will increase, and the demand for vehicles to commute or escape will decline.
- The construction industry will change dramatically. The demand for suburban houses behind fences will decline. People will be seeking urban development and housing styles that are more supportive of community life.

The Kingdom of God has come when all the authority is freely submitted to Jesus. Most authority in the modern world resides in businesses. The business world contains far more authority than the church. All this authority will be surrendered to Jesus as the Holy Spirit works in the hearts of business managers and owners, and they freely choose to serve him. When they freely surrender, other believers will teach them how to serve and obey him.

Cooperation not Corporation

In the modern world, limited liability and other corporate laws have allowed businesses to become very large with enormous hierarchies of power. These huge conglomerates provide great opportunities for the powers of darkness. They concentrate their efforts on the senior management because it gives them control over vast resources. Power managers tend to have big egos, so these power plays by the spiritual powers of evil are usually successful.

Corporate structures will be different in the Kingdom of God. Large conglomerates will not be viable because the risks will be too high without government protection. Growth for the sake of growth will not be practical. Big corporations will be replaced by numerous smaller businesses cooperating to achieve the same purpose.

The benefit of the big corporate model is the ability to control immense resources and complex processes, but hierarchy is the devil's home. He works through manipulation and control of a big hierarchy, whereas Jesus spreads authority around and relies on the Holy Spirit to coordinate people to achieve a common purpose.

Many businesses aim to get bigger, so they can destroy their opposition. This is unnecessary in God's economy. We have a big God, who does not need big business. As business conglomerates shrink and disappear, control and domination will be replaced by relationships, cooperation and contracts.

A business that operates a large, complicated, resource-intensive series of processes will not be able to bring every aspect of production under its control as the risks will be too large. Instead of owning and controlling every aspect of the production process, it will be managed through contracts with numerous suppliers and service providers. The role of the business will change from controlling everything to coordinating and managing relationships with a network of supporting businesses.

The modern economy is dominated by large businesses protected by human governments. In the Kingdom of God, businesses will be smaller and more numerous and the networks between them more important. Authoritarian executives with the big egos that control enormous corporations for super-salaries will be replaced by good people who can manage cooperation with other businesses for a fair reward.

Family Business

When human government disappears, big business will fade away. As the gospel advances, families will have a much bigger role in the business world.

- Family business is important for training and developing talents. Working together in a business is a good way for parents to train their children. Parents who are skilled at business will replicate their ministry in their children.
- Family ties are strengthened by shared business activities. Resources will be available for supporting family members who face hardships.
- A family business will often be centred in their Kingdom Community. As local communities are restored, entrepreneurs will look for opportunities to start businesses that strengthen relationships within their community.
- The owners of a family business should employ some people from outside their family. Even if the employee is not a follower of Jesus, they will have to acknowledge their employer's authority while they are working in the business.
- Small businesses will predominate in the Kingdom of God. Big business aims to control broad areas of economic activity. The Kingdom way will be numerous smaller businesses joined together by a network of relationships and contracts.
- Some very complicated tasks will need larger businesses.

God prefers family businesses. As the Kingdom of God advances, many large businesses will be chopped up and spread around. Smaller family-owned businesses will abound. The Kingdom of God has more potential in businesses that are owned by a family or small group of people who trust each other. If they choose to serve Jesus, they can transform the culture of their business.

Challenge and Opportunity

The globalisation of business has produced unprecedented wealth and supplied a fantastic range of cheap consumer goods. This prosperity could last forever, but it is more likely that globalisation will collapse under the pressures of political power struggles, declining empires, failing governments, financial crisis, or war.

- Business models that rely on global supply chains will fail.
- If the modern financial system collapses, the funding that multi-national businesses rely on will disappear.
- Opportunities for specialisation will be significantly reduced.
- Many people will lose employment as the global supply chain breaks down.
- Demand for many trivial goods and services will disappear as people focus more on their basic needs.
- More of the goods and services that people need will have to be produced locally.

These changes will be a serious challenge, but they will also be a great opportunity for those who are alert and prepared. Christian entrepreneurs should be ready to take up this challenge. Networks of relationships between churches will ensure that goods and services flow from those who are skilled at producing them to the people who need them.

While the good times last, we should be preparing for the challenges that lie ahead. Many important areas of human activity have been taken over by the spirit of the world. As the gospel is proclaimed in the power of the Spirit and the Kingdom of God comes to fullness, these activities will need to be restored by bringing their authority into alignment with God's will.

- Education
- Banking
- Entertainment
- Culture, arts and media
- Healthcare

Christians must not seize control of these activities and impose their will on them. Rather, they should humbly serve their communities and display the fruit of God's economic wisdom.

Jesus' followers must not take back authority by force. They should not impose their authority on unwilling people. They should only take up authority that is freely submitted to them.

Members of Kingdom Communities should establish new businesses that provide these services for the glory of God and according to his will. Inspired by the Spirit, they will find ways to do these tasks better than the world. At first, these businesses will be small, and often hidden, but when the opportunity arises, they will be ready to expand and grow as the Spirit leads. When human governments collapse, they will be ready to fill the gap.

Kingdom communities will provide economic support for people who lose their jobs and income. Unemployment will be less of a problem in a community that is giving and sharing.

Kingdom Communities must be prepared for distress and equipped for victory. By getting rid of unrighteous wealth, escaping from the clutches of debt, and loving one another through giving and sharing, followers of Jesus will be prepared to survive through any economic crisis that occurs. By learning to do business according to God's will, they will be equipped for that glorious season when the governments of the world become the government of our God and his Messiah Jesus, who will reign forever.

13
Savings and Investment

Saving is essential for the flourishing of life. To understand why, consider a subsistence fisherman. He has no equipment, but he catches enough fish with his wooden spear to survive by working most of the day. He could improve his fishing by making some nets and a boat, but while he was doing it, he would not have time to fish so he would go hungry. If he could save a little bit of fish each day, he can build up a stock of saved fish, which he can live on while he builds a net and boat.

With the net and boat (his productive equipment) he can catch enough fish to live on in half a day. This means that he will only need to fish every second day. He can use the other day to make better equipment or other things that will improve his lifestyle. Or he could fish every day and trade the surplus with other people for other things that he needs. Productive equipment gives the fisherman a better lifestyle because he can catch more fish.

Productive Equipment
Economists distinguish between "capital goods" and "consumption goods". The word "capital" is used to describe goods that can be used to produce other goods. A spade is a capital good. You cannot eat it if you are hungry, but you can use it to produce food. Capital goods include machinery and factories.

Consumer goods satisfy human wants and needs. They cannot be used to produce other goods. A banana is a consumer good. You cannot use it to make things, but it will satisfy your hunger. Some goods are both capital and consumption goods. When a computer is used to design machinery, it is a capital good. When children play games on a computer, it becomes a consumption good.

The word "capital" has too many meanings to be useful. It sometimes refers to a sum of money available for investment. Economists use the name "capital" for plant and machinery. The large corporations that dominate the capitalist system are often called "capital." Mixing up these meanings creates confusion, so I avoid the word. I prefer the expression "productive equipment" because it is clear what is being described. It includes all forms of technology, machinery equipment and factories.

In Jesus time, oxen, donkeys, fishing boats, nets, builders' tools and cooking utensils made people more productive in their work.

> Your basket and your kneading trough will be blessed (Deut 28:5).

Baskets and kneading troughs are productive equipment. Oxen assisted with food production.

> Where there are no oxen, the manger is empty, but from the strength of an ox come abundant harvests (Prov 14:4).

God blesses productive equipment and technology that is acquired honestly and used wisely.

During the industrial revolution, productive equipment became more complicated. Labour-saving tools and machines replaced hard physical work. Even greater benefit came when employees were provided with highly technical equipment that enhanced their skills. As technology improved, productive equipment could be manufactured using electronically-controlled machines, which made it even more productive.

Modern productive equipment draws on externally-generated power and uses sophisticated technology. It includes factories, information technology, robots and transport equipment. But the principle is the same. Productive equipment and technology make people more productive.

How?

Productive equipment can be obtained in several ways.

- **Make** - In traditional societies productive equipment is made by the people who use it. Fishermen made their own nets.
- **Steal** - Throughout history, stealing productive equipment from the person who made it has been a common way to get it. This is forbidden by the Instructions for Economic Life.
- **Save** - In the modern world, the most common way to obtain productive equipment is to save money and buy it.
- **Borrow** – Borrowing to buy productive equipment uses the savings of other people.
- **Inherit** - Productive equipment can have a long life, so people sometimes inherit it from their parents. That is legitimate provided it is not unrighteous wealth.

In each of these options, someone made savings that allowed the productive equipment to be produced.

Savings

Getting some productive equipment improved the quality of the fisherman's life. However, to obtain the boat and the net, he first had to make some savings. He had to save a supply of fish to live on while he was building his boat and making his net. The reward for consuming less and saving was the stream of extra income he was able to produce with his productive equipment.

The same principle applies to any economy. If all income is spent on consumption goods, there will be nothing left to buy productive equipment. To make or buy productive equipment someone has to forgo consumption. Developing new technology takes time, so savings are needed to sustain it. The reward for giving up consumption is an increase in production.

Some economists are hostile to savings because they believe that consumption drives the economy. They have it the wrong way around. Savings support investment in productive equipment and technology, which increases the productivity of the economy. The increase in production allows greater consumption.

Economic development occurs when the stock of productive equipment in the economy is developed. This can only happen if someone in the economy saves.

Saving and Investment

All productive assets originate with someone saving. Savings can be converted into productive assets in three different ways.

- Buying productive equipment and operating a business.
- Lending the savings to a business that needs new equipment.
- Buying shares in a business that is raising funds to buy new technology and equipment.

The way that the saver gets rewarded for deferring their consumption depends on which of these channels is chosen.

- A business should produce a profit.
- A productive loan earns interest.
- Shares earn dividends (or an increased price).

Provided savings are channelled into the purchase of productive equipment, the saver gets a reward for deferring their consumption.

A new loan can only be made if someone has saved what is being lent. Someone has to forgo spending so that another person can spend what they have not earned by getting a loan. Lending without saving produces inflation.

Investing in the Future

As people living in Kingdom Communities learn to support each other, savings for unforeseen circumstances, such as sickness, accident, and death will become less important. Most of these needs will be met by caring and sharing within the community.

Thrift will produce a surplus of resources that are available for investment in productive activities. This investment will make everyone more productive. Healthy businesses will strengthen the community and be an inheritance for the families of the thrifty.

Some savings will be loaned to businesses. The productive equipment purchased with a loan will produce a return to the borrower, which should cover the cost of any interest. However, as the Kingdom of God advances and blessing flows, most businesses should quickly become debt free. Business expansion will mostly be financed from retained earnings or by selling equity.

Most of the surplus that is saved in a Kingdom Community will be invested in businesses that contribute to the strength of their community. Savings will mostly be channelled into equity, not debt.

Followers of Jesus should seek the guidance of the Holy Spirit when deciding what to do with their savings. They will usually give to people in need or invest their surplus funds into enterprises that will be productive for the Kingdom of God. By operating their own business, or owning shares in a good business, they can ensure that their savings are used for the glory of God.

Falling Prices

If an economy is investing in productive equipment and implementing new technology (and governments and banks are not inflating the currency), prices should be slowly falling as rising productivity makes production processes more efficient. A few prices might increase in response to shifts in demand, but the prices of most goods and services will fall, as new technology and economies of scale reduce the costs of production.

Declining prices are a powerful economic mechanism because the benefits flow to everyone in the economy. People on fixed incomes benefit because the things they have to buy get cheaper. Those who are weak and powerless benefit because they can purchase more with what they have. Inflation benefits the few who can work the system and know how to use debt to speculate in property. Falling prices benefit everyone in the economy.

When governments allow banks to inflate the currency, the benefits of increased productivity are captured by those with economic and political power, because they can negotiate increases in income to compensate. Even if price inflation is low, poor people become worse off because they don't have sufficient political power to negotiate increases in their incomes to compensate. Eliminating inflation assists people who are poor.

Investment in productive equipment usually reduces prices. The poor benefit without any need to negotiate increases in income.

Inequality

Humanistic capitalism has solved the production problem. It has allowed human initiative and inventiveness to flourish. The accumulation of productive assets has massively increased human productivity. Trade has supported increased specialisation and productivity. These changes have moved us from a life of subsistence to a world of prosperity in a few centuries.

I dislike the word "capitalism". It is used in many ways, so it is not always clear what it means. More seriously, modern capitalism is an ugly mix of corporate control, political power, a burgeoning debt industry, bleeding debt, rampant military force and civil religion, all glued together by fanatical nationalism that has tarnished the word beyond redemption.

The problem with humanistic capitalism is that productive wealth tends to be concentrated in the hands of a few.

- Productive equipment makes people more productive so those who own it increase their wealth.
- Efficient entrepreneurs are rewarded with increasing wealth. This is legitimate. Most use the increase in wealth to expand their enterprise.
- Some wealth trickles down to those at the bottom, but the flow up is much greater.
- Poor people struggle to make the savings needed to obtain productive equipment.
- When wealthy people collude with political rulers, the flow of wealth to the rich and powerful is really boosted.

Humanistic capitalism can increase the wealth of most people in society, but it massively increases inequality. This inequality becomes a festering sore that weakens society. Secular economists have come up with two solutions to inequality.

- The most popular solution to inequality is progressive taxation. This solution is immoral. There is no basis in the Instructions for Economic Life for confiscating the wealth of the rich and giving it to the poor.
- The other solution is revolution: shoot the rich and let the poor grab what they can. This solution is immoral and

destructive. Revolutions usually destroy an economy, which leaves everyone worse off.

Both these solutions to inequality are wrong and have usually failed.

Sharing Productive Equipment

Markets do not distribute capital equipment equally because they reward successful entrepreneurs with increased wealth. Through the normal working of the market, some people will accumulate wealth as they make good decisions and others will lose their wealth through mistakes or adverse circumstances.

The land laws of the Old Testament provided a solution to inequality that was very effective in an agrarian economy where land was the main form of wealth. The land was distributed evenly among all families. If someone became poor and sold their land, the buyer had to return it to them at the next jubilee. The return of land was voluntary and the jubilee laws were not enforced by the state. Voluntarily fulfilment of the jubilee ensured that land remained with families and its distribution remained roughly equal.

In the modern world, where other forms of productive asset are far more important than land, giving and sharing will be necessary to ensure that they are evenly distributed. Jesus gave a solution to the problems caused by lack of productive assets.

> Sell your possessions and give to the poor. Provide purses
> for yourselves that will not wear out, a treasure in heaven
> that will never fail (Luke 12:33).

Those who have plenty of productive equipment should give to those with none. The outcome will be greater equality (2 Cor 8:14).

When helping people to give away unrighteous wealth, deacons should channel productive assets to poor people who have the capability to use them responsibly to be more productive. Christians should train up potential recipients, so they know how to use their productive equipment wisely and not dissipate it in pointless consumption.

Radical sharing is the key to removing inequality, particularly sharing of productive equipment. Transferring productive assets to the poor by giving and sharing will move society closer to equality.

People with wealth should seek out ways to provide productive equipment for those who do not have enough.

- Giving interest-free loans to those who are poor.
- Giving surplus productive equipment to people who can use it effectively.
- Giving poor people shares in their business.
- Employing poor people and providing them with productive equipment to assist them to earn more.
- Assisting employees to get enough productive equipment to start a business.

Jacob and Laban were shifty operators, so we should not copy their lifestyle, but they are a good example of one person helping another to build up their productive assets. When Jacob went to live with Laban, he owned nothing. Laban capitalised Jacob's wages by paying him with breeding ewes (Gen 29,30). Jacob was able to build up his own flock without neglecting Laban's. This was an early form of share-farming.

A more equal distribution of productive equipment will dramatically reduce poverty. The prophet Isaiah looked forward to a time when every person would own some productive equipment.

> They will build houses and dwell in them;
> they will plant vineyards and eat their fruit.
> No longer will they build houses and others live in them,
> or plant and others eat (Is 65:21-22).

Micah had a similar vision.

> Every man will sit under his own vine and under his own
> fig tree, and no one will make them afraid (Mic 4:4).

Everyone in the Kingdom Economy will own some productive equipment, so they will be able to provide for themselves. Wise giving and sharing can make this happen.

14

Interest

The payment of interest has been a controversial topic for Christians. Some say that charging interest is wrong. For much of history, it was referred to as usury. This was the result of a misunderstanding of the Old Testament teaching on loans to the poor. It distinguishes between poor loans and business loans.

The Old Testament prohibits interest on loans to the poor because they are a way of loving a neighbour.

> If you lend money to any of my people who are poor among you, you shall not be like a moneylender to him; you shall not charge him interest (Ex 22:25).

> If any of your fellow Israelites become poor and are unable to support themselves, help them... Do not take interest or any profit from them... You must not lend them money at interest or sell them food at a profit (Lev 25: 35-37).

A poor person uses the money they have borrowed for consumption goods, so they get no profit to pay interest. Charging them interest would be wrong, as it would produce unrighteous wealth.

This prohibition on charging interest on loans to the poor was erroneously extended to business loans by Christians. Interest on commercial loans for use in trade or business is not forbidden in the Instructions for Economic Life, although debt is discouraged.

Stuck in Time

Our relationship with time is the reason for charging interest. Interest is the fee paid to people who postpone the purchase of goods and services that they are entitled to buy. We live in the present, so people mostly prefer something they can consume now to something they might be able to consume in the future. Today seems better than next year, so savers need to be compensated for postponing their consumption.

The present is always more certain than the future. Goods available in the present will be worth more than those available in the future. Interest rates reflect this difference. Interest is the compensation that savers get for postponing their purchases until a later date and accepting the risk that inflation might erode the value of future repayments.

Looking from the other side, interest is the price borrowers pay for making purchases sooner than they would normally be able to. Most people dislike waiting for something that they cannot have now. They are willing to pay extra to bring their purchase of goods from the future into the present.

Interest is unavoidable because we are finite people living in the present with a view of the future. We can think about the future, but we have to act in the present. Interest is a fact of life, because we can plan for the future, but must act in the present. A consequence of our temporality is that a purchase in the present is worth more than one in the future. The payment of interest reflects the reality that the present is certain, whereas the future is uncertain.

Buying and selling occurs in the present because a sale occurs when buyer and seller agree on a price. There is no time dimension, so interest cannot be charged. In contrast, saving, lending and borrowing shift purchases through time between the present and the future. Once time is involved, the difference in value between the present and the future makes interest appropriate.

Jesus left his place with his Father in eternity and came to earth and lived as a man, so the constraints of time were real for him. He illustrated his understanding of the value of time in his parable of the talents. Giving up the use of money for a period of time has a cost, even if the money is just buried in the ground (Matt 25:14-27).

If Jim borrows $1000 from Bill to buy a new machine for his business and freely agrees to pay back $1500 at the end of seven years, theft has not occurred. This interest payment is Bill's reward for postponing his consumption for seven years. Jim is willing to pay back more than he borrowed, as the loan will enable him to buy a new machine that his business needs to prosper.

Once production gets complicated, time shifting becomes very important. When a car or a laptop is being manufactured, design has to begin long before one can be sold. Parts have to be designed and ordered several months before they are used. Once manufactured, the components have to be shipped to the place where they will be assembled. Once the assembly process is complete, the final product has to be shipped to where it will be sold. The process from design to sale takes considerable time.

The cost of these shifts across time can be funded with equity, but borrowing and lending at interest is an equally valid way to finance them. In a complex production situation, borrowing with interest supports time shifting without anyone being harmed.

Interest is a Price

Interest is not something sinister; it is just a price. Prices are just information about offers made and accepted. They contain information that is useful to other buyers and sellers. Prices are technical, not moral. Most of the time they are useful information.

A high price during a famine is evil, but it is the person demanding the high price that is wrong, not the price itself. The high price is just a sign of their bad behaviour. If someone lies to get a high price, it is the lying that is morally wrong, not the price. Only actions by people can be moral.

Interest is the price for the service of bringing the future into the present. It is the price paid to get something now instead of waiting until later. People shift the future into the present all the time. It is not always wise, but it is legitimate activity provided it is done honestly without duress.

The moral behaviour of the two people agreeing to a transaction for a price can be good or evil. There are situations where charging interest is morally wrong. Otherwise, if both parties to the transaction agree to the rate of interest and the term of the loan without intimidation or pressure, it is legitimate.

Limitations on Interest

The Instructions for Economic Life specify two situations where interest must not be charged on loans.

- Charging interest to vulnerable people is morally wrong. The instructions for Economic Life require God's people to provide interest-free loans to people that are poor (Ex 22:25; Deut 23:19-20). These loans are to be cancelled after seven years if the person is unable to repay the loan.

  When a poor person is offered an interest-free loan, the interest cost is not eliminated. Rather, it shifts from the borrower to the lender, who accepts it as the cost of the gift. Jesus urged his followers to make interest free loans because he understood that this cost could put some people off. Unfortunately, many Christians have avoided the cost of forgoing interest, by refusing to make loans to the poor.

- Charging interest is also forbidden on loans to brothers and sisters. God's people can only charge interest to strangers.

  > To a stranger you may charge interest, but to your brother you shall not charge interest, that the Lord your God may bless you in everything you set your hand to in the land (Deut 23:20).

  In the New Testament age, this applies to brothers and sisters in the Lord. Followers of Jesus are required to love one another, so they should be willing to lend to each other without requiring interest.

  Followers of Jesus can charge interest to strangers. A business organisation is a stranger, not a brother, even if some of the owners or managers are Christians, so charging interest on a business loan is legitimate. We are not required to give interest-free loans to business organisations. They should carry the cost of the debt, not the lender. If the decision to take a loan is wise, the business should be able to pay the cost.

Christians must not demand interest-free loans from other believers. An interest-free loan is a gift because the cost is real. A gift must not be made into a rule. We should be generous because we are motivated by love, not by emotional pressure to keep a rule
.

Investment Decisions

Savings and investment are related, but decisions about them are usually made by different actors in the economy. Investment decisions are made by entrepreneurs and businesses, whereas savings decisions are usually made by people and households.

The link between these independent actors is the interest rate. If interest rates are low many business projects will be viable, but savings could be insufficient to fund them. If interest rates rise, people will save more, but some projects that were viable at the low interest rate will no longer be profitable, ie the supply of funds increases while the demand will decline.

If interest rates are too high, savings will be plentiful, but very few investment projects will be viable. When interest rates fall, more potential projects become economic, so businesses and entrepreneurs will invest more, absorbing the surplus saving. This investment will make the economy more productive.

If governments are not fiddling with interest rates and banks are not creating credit, interest rates should adjust to clear the market by ensuring that savings are matched by equivalent investments.

The payment of interest supports economic growth. If business loans do not earn interest, people will have less incentive to save. The only people who would save are those who can invest in a business directly. Most others would just consume all they earn. The resulting shortage of productive equipment and lack of technology could limit the growth of the economy.

Distortion

Modern governments control interest rates to prevent inflation of their nation's currency. Controlling the supply of money is almost impossible, so most governments now authorise a central bank to set interest rates to achieve an inflation target. The problem is that interest rates are an important market signal for businesses and households making economic decisions.

If the central bank sets interest rates too low, entrepreneurs will invest in products that are not truly viable and banks are tempted to fund property speculation. If rates are set too high, many potential projects will be unprofitable. Investment will slow and productivity will decline. Interest rates influence many economic decisions. Allowing a central bank to set interest rates is a mistake, as they usually get the level wrong. Economic decision-makers get distorted information, which leads to poor economic performance.

Loss of Hope

Interest is a reward for deferring consumption to a later time, so the level of interest rates is mostly determined by the value that people place on the future. When people live for the present with no hope for the future, interest rates rise. High rates are the sign of a sick culture. On the other hand, if people are confident in the future, they will need less compensation for saving, so rates will be lower (provided government intervention does not distort them).

The new century has brought a radical change in worldview. Most people now live for the moment. Hope has died and the future has become a source of fear and dread. Music, literature, television and films have become an escape from the future rather than a source of hope.

Without faith in God, there is no hope, so the humanistic hope that dominated the twentieth century was an aberration. Society is now living in a way that is more consistent with its presuppositions. As the Apostle Paul says, if there is no resurrection, "Let us eat, drink and be merry because tomorrow we die". Living in the moment is normal in a society without God, so saving for the future will not be very popular. High-interest rates will be needed to persuade people to save.

If banks were not free to create credit, interest rates would have soared in the modern world. This would have reduced investment in productive assets. A focus on consumption can destroy a nation's wealth. If living for the present becomes too intense, productive equipment will often be destroyed to finance consumption in the present. This would slow economic growth. Societies that consume all that they produce become poor.

> There is desirable treasure and oil in the dwelling of the wise,
> but a foolish man squanders it (Prov 21:20).

Citizens of the Kingdom of God should be thrifty. Steady saving will enable them to build up their productive assets.

In God's economy, interest rates will be determined by lenders and borrowers, not a central bank or government. If savings are scarce, interest rates will rise. If they are abundant, rates will fall.

As the gospel advances, high levels of thrift and declining demand for loans will cause interest rates to fall. The sound banking system that emerges in the Kingdom Economy will eliminate inflation, so savers would not need extra interest to compensate them for rising prices. As honesty increases, the extra margin for risk will reduce. The Kingdom Economy will boost confidence in the future causing interest rates to fall.

Compound Interest

When a culture is absorbed in enjoying the present, people are tempted to borrow to increase their consumption. Interest makes this a risky practice because once the goods purchased have been consumed the borrower has nothing left to repay the loan or interest. They come under pressure to borrow more to pay the interest owed. This is unwise because they usually have no way to escape from compounding interest charges.

The compounding of interest is a serious problem in the modern world. When a bank pays compound interest on a deposit, it adds the interest to the deposit rather than paying it out. This is not wrong in itself, because savers are entitled to save their interest if it was earned from productive lending.

From a borrower's perspective, paying compound interest is borrowing to pay interest. This is unwise for a business because it should be trying to decrease debt rather than increase it. For a person borrowing to fund consumption, increasing their debt to pay interest is very foolish, because they are making themselves a slave to debt.

Everyone would like to be able to increase their consumption in the present without needing to work harder, but interest reminds us that living for the present at the expense of the future has a real cost. If followers of Jesus are content with what they have, they will not need to borrow to increase their consumption. Being content will keep them from the trap of compound interest.

Rich people like compound interest because it makes their money grow fast. With compound interest at 6 percent, their savings will double in about twelve years. Compound interest speeds the shift of wealth from the rich to the poor.

Interest can only be added to the money already deposited if the bank can lend the additional savings to someone else. Therefore, savers can only double their money every twelve years using compound interest if the level of debt in society doubles at the same time. Compound interest is only possible in an economy that is becoming increasingly indebted. Without a government enforcing the repayment of debt, this could not happen.

In a society where the gospel is advancing by the power of the Holy Spirit, compound interest will not be possible, because people will be reducing their debts. If the bank adds the interest earned each quarter to the deposit they hold, they will have difficulty finding someone to borrow the extra money. They will need to reduce their interest rates to attract new borrowers, so the speed at which deposits can grow will be squeezed.

Be Content

In a Kingdom Community, most people will be content with what they have, so lending will be limited to productive loans. Poor people will be able to get interest-free loans to get out of trouble. Most others will be thrifty and wait to buy the things they want, so plentiful savings will push interest rates down. Savers will be forced to look for different more-productive investments.

Part 3

Better Money and Banking

The first two chapters of Part Three describe the problems with modern money and banking. Followers of Jesus need to understand these problems, but they do not prevent them from living out God's Instructions for Economic Life within their Kingdom Communities.

The flaws of money and banking inevitably produce economic instability, inequality and often extreme poverty. The entire financial structure is so weighed down by debt that it will likely collapse. If that happens, God's people must be ready with better institutions to offer a world that is desperate for a robust alternative.

Not everyone is called to this task, but the last three chapters of Part 3 explain how better money and better financial institutions can be established within Kingdom Communities ready for the season when the world is ready for them. I give examples to illustrate the application of the Instructions for Economic Life, but those with this calling will need to work out the detail in their own culture and society by following the leading of the Holy Spirit.

Part 3 is quite technical. Readers who find it too complicated are free to ignore it. They should find plenty to ponder in the first two parts.

15
Money

Everyone is better off, if people can specialise in what they do best. Most people will produce more than they need of what they do well and exchange it for other things that they need. This division of labour allows people to be more productive and the economy to be more efficient. For this to occur, people must be able to freely buy and sell the goods and services they have produced.

Some people will be able to swap their surplus with people who have what they want, but this is very inefficient. People would waste time looking for someone with whom to swap. Often it will not be possible to find a person with a surplus of what I want, who wants what I have. The person with a surplus of what I want will often want something different from what I have.

Money provides a solution to this problem. If I can find someone who wants what I have, I can swap it for money and use the money to buy what I need from the person who has it. Money enables people to sell their surplus production and buy the goods and services that they need from other people.

Distance Gap
To understand how a sound money system should function, we need to understand its nature. Money improves our lives by simplifying buying and selling of goods and services.

Most people cannot produce everything that they will need to live. Most buy the goods and services that they want from other people or businesses. They pay for them by selling goods that they own or by working for someone else. However, the people that they sell to or work for will usually not have the things that they want. They will need to buy what they want from another person or business. They cannot buy and sell simultaneously.

Buying and selling will often occur in different places, with different people, at different times. There will be a distance and time gap between selling and buying. I will often have to hand over what I am selling to the buyer before I can go to the seller that has the goods or services that I want. Once I have handed over what I had to a purchaser, I need proof that I made the sale and am entitled to get what I need from someone else. Money solves this problem.

Money is evidence of a half-completed transaction

Money is evidence that I have completed half a transaction by doing work or giving up goods and services to someone in my society and am entitled to complete the transaction by getting the goods and services I need from someone else in society.

From an individual point of view, every transaction has two parts. In the first part, I sell something, which I no longer want, in exchange for money. However, I don't want money. I want something else that I can use. I use the money to buy the thing that I really want. Buying is the second part of the transaction.

Undertaking half a transaction without evidence, in the hope that I can persuade someone to give something back would be risky. The person who has what I want might be unwilling to give it to me without some proof of my claim that I have completed half a transaction. To avoid this risk, I only give up goods as the first half of a transaction if I receive money in return. Then I have proof that I have completed half a transaction and have a valid entitlement to goods from someone else.

Money supports trade by providing a link between the first part of the transaction and the second part of the transaction. When I sell my goods, I accept money in return, because I can use the money to get what I want to complete the transaction. I start with something I did not want. I end up with something that I wanted more. The money is my security for the short gap between the first part of the transaction and the second part.

> *Money is a record of a claim that other people in my society recognise and accept.*

Social Acceptance

The usefulness of money depends on it being accepted by other people. We accept money when we work or sell things because we know that other people will take it in exchange for the goods or services we want from them.

People accept money as payment for work because they know other people will give up goods and services in return for it. A seller can accept money from the person who wants what they have, knowing that they can use the money to get what they want from other people. Money is useful for completing a transaction because we know that everyone in our society will accept it.

The fact that the person who buys from me has money proves that they have completed half of a transaction by giving up goods and services to someone else and is entitled to mine. People who have not produced and sold anything will not have money, so they will not be entitled to buy any goods and services.

A socially acceptable method for demonstrating that half a transaction has been completed is essential for the expansion of trade. Money is a widely accepted way of proving that a person is entitled to complete their transaction by obtaining goods and services from someone in society.

The possession of money is a sign to other people in the society that a seller has completed half of his transaction, by giving up something. It allows them to buy something from someone else to complete the transaction.

Money is a socially-accepted record of a half-completed transaction. It demonstrates that I have given up goods and services to someone in my society and have not yet completed the other half of the transaction and received some back from any other member of my society.

The Risk of Holding Money

Holding money is risky. Once I have handed over my thing to the buyer, I cannot get it back, but I cannot be certain that I will be able to buy the thing that I want with the money. If no one accepts the money in exchange for what I want, I will be left with nothing useful (I did not want money). Once I have made my purchase, the risk is gone because I have the thing I wanted. The risk has passed to the person who takes the money from me.

Money does not guarantee that I will receive back the same value that I have given up. I bear the risk that prices will change between the time when I give up my goods or services in exchange for money and when I use the money to purchase goods or services from someone else. If prices have risen, I may not be able to obtain goods or services of the same value to me as those I gave up. Of course, if prices have fallen, I may gain additional value.

The risk of loss is greater if there is a big time-gap between selling and buying. However, if I hold money, I am confident that I can buy goods and services, provided I can find someone willing to sell at a price agreeable to me.

Reliable money is so critical for economic development. Trade will only expand if this risk of holding money is relatively low. If the risks are too high, then people will tend to make do with what they have, rather than attempt to sell it and buy something better.

Dishonest Money

Human societies have developed various forms of money to record their half-completed transactions. The problem with most of these methods is that dishonest people, merchants and banks found ways to create money that did not represent half-completed transactions. Their dishonest money enabled people to purchase things without giving up anything in return. Dishonest money is theft.

Once it became clear that merchants and banks could not be trusted to maintain honest money, kings and government got in on the act. Unfortunately, trusting governments to provide honest money is like asking a fox to guard a henhouse. Kings and governments frequently colluded with banks to create money that did not represent half-completed transactions.

God wants honest money. A method for recording half-completed transactions that complies with the Instruction for Economic Life is outlined in chapter 17. In the remainder of this chapter, I briefly describe the problems that come when governments try to manipulate and control the money system.

Inflation is Theft

When banks, kings or governments create new money that does not represent half-completed transactions, the volume of money in the economy increases but nothing extra is produced. Inflation is the inevitable consequence, because with nothing extra to buy, the additional money in circulation pushes up prices. Ordinary people suffer because the money they have accepted in good faith as a record of half-completed transactions lose its value.

State control of the money supply is supposed to eliminate inflation, but it usually makes the situation worse. Rampant inflation has undermined the economies of many nations. Economic history is littered with examples of kings and governments who devastated the economy of their nation by inflating their currency to pay for their wars and rash promises.

Many economists claim that a little inflation is good because it encourages people to make purchases. Governments and politicians like inflation because it increases tax receipts with any change in tax rates. Debtors like inflation because it shrinks the value of what they owe. However, inflation hurts people on fixed incomes and punishes savers, because it slowly erodes the value of savings.

Governments that allow inflation of their currency are supporting theft. The Old Testament prophets condemned kings and rulers who destroy their currency through inflation.

> Your silver has become dross...
> Your rulers are rebels
> and companions of thieves (Is 1:22,23).

In God's eyes, kings and government who undermine the value of their nation's currency are the companions of thieves.

Many central banks manipulate interest rates to achieve an inflation target of two or three percent per year, but this robs innocent people of their wealth. If prices increase at these rates, the value of their savings will be halved in about fifteen years. After thirty years of "normal" inflation, the savings of a responsible person would be close to worthless. Inflation is disguised theft.

Bank Problem

Most modern governments license banks and establish the rules under which they must operate. Unfortunately, banking laws have allowed an insidious form of dishonest money to emerge. In most countries, banking regulations allow banks to treat their customers' deposits as their own assets. This practice enables them to create money that does not represent half-completed transactions. The ability of banks to create money is a serious moral and economic problem. (The process is complicated, so I devote the whole of the next chapter to describing it).

16
Banks

Bad Accounting

Over the centuries, people have used a variety of methods for recording their half-completed transaction. In the modern world, most money is an electronic record on the computer system of the bank. This is efficient, but bank regulators have permitted banks to use unsound accounting practices that allow them to create money. Creation of additional money causes inflation and increases the instability of the economy.

The basic problem is that modern banking regulations allow banks to lend money that has been deposited on call. This money is put into the bank for safekeeping until it is needed. Money deposited on call can be withdrawn whenever the depositor chooses. A problem with the way that these transactions are recorded in the accounts of the bank allows them to lend money that should not be lent.

The best way to illustrate this problem is with an example. When I get paid, my salary goes into my cheque account. I am not lending my salary to the bank, because I will spend most of it in the next fortnight before I get again paid. I want to be able to spend my money whenever I choose, for whatever I want to buy, so I choose a bank account that is available on demand.

When my salary goes into the bank, I have not transferred ownership of that money to the bank. The money is mine. It does not belong to the bank. However, the current accounting process used by banks records the money it has received as an asset and its responsibility to me as a liability. This is wrong. The money does not belong to the bank. It belongs to me, so it should be an asset on my balance sheet, not an asset on the bank's accounts.

Warehouse

An asset cannot have two owners. A parallel example makes this clear. If I am going out of town for a while, I may engage a warehouse to store my dining suite until I return. The warehouse will charge a fee for providing this service. When my dining suite goes into the warehouse, its ownership does not change. The dining suite still belongs to me.

The warehouse owner cannot do what he likes with the table. He cannot bring it out and use it when he has guests for dinner. He cannot dance on the tabletop or use it for playing table tennis. The warehouse owner cannot decide how the table will be used, because he has no ownership rights to it. He has a duty to care for my dining table in the way specified in the contract.

If I decide not to return, I can write to the warehouse and ask that the table be delivered to my daughter and the chairs to one of my friends. The warehouse owner will do this, provided I pay the cost of transport. He cannot refuse to carry out my request, because he has relatives staying and is using the table. If this happened, I would accuse him of stealing my dining suite. If he has moved it to his own home, I could accuse him of theft. Everyone would understand that he has done wrong.

If the word got out about what he had done, his warehouse would soon be empty, because people would stop trusting him. The service that he offers is skill at caring for things that belong to other people. This service only has value to customers, if they can trust him to provide the care that he has promised. He is really selling trust, so if he proves to be untrustworthy, his service loses value and people will be unwilling to pay for it.

The warehouse owner does not record the things stored in his warehouse on his balance sheet. The only asset on his balance sheet will be the warehouse that he owns. He does not include the contents of the warehouse, because they are not his assets.

Modern Banks

When I put my salary in the bank, I am really just putting it in a warehouse for safekeeping. I also use the bank because it allows me to make payments to other people, by cheque or electronic transfer.

I am clear about one thing. My money belongs to me, even when it is in the bank. I want to be able to spend it when I choose. It is my asset, so it does not belong to the bank. Therefore, the bank should not record my money on its balance sheet as an asset. My money does not belong to the bank. It is simply storing my money like a warehouse stores furniture.

The heart of the problem with the modern banking system is that banks claim ownership of the money that has been deposited by their customers. They record this money as an asset on their balance sheet. They treat the money as if they owned it. This is problematic because the money now has two owners. I think that I own it, while the bank acts as if it owns it.

Two owners

Having an asset with two owners might be fine for a while if the real owner does not want to use the asset immediately. However, problems will eventually arise. If the owners of money in the bank want to withdraw it and the bank has done something else with the money, the conflict is obvious. If too many people want to withdraw at the same time, a bank run could occur and the bank might default on its obligations.

The withdrawal problem does not arise with a warehouse. If all the people with furniture stored in a warehouse decided to take it out on the same day, it would not matter. The warehouse owner would be very busy responding to customers, and he might be worried about his future income, but every person could get back what they owned. Banks should be the same.

The solution to this is quite clear. If the warehouse owner claimed ownership of the stuff stored in his warehouse, he would be accused of theft. If a bank claims ownership of money entrusted to it for care, the same applies. It has taken ownership of something that does not belong to it.

The Bible is clear that a thing cannot have two owners. If two people claim the same thing, judges should resolve the dispute.

> In all cases of illegal possession of an ox, a donkey, a sheep, a garment, or any other lost property about which somebody says, 'This is mine,' both parties are to bring their cases before the judges. The one whom the judges declare guilty must pay back double to his neighbour (Ex 22:9).

If I say of my deposit, "This is mine" and the bank is also saying, "This is mine", something is wrong. This is an issue that could be resolved by judges. They would find that the bank has claimed something that does not belong to it, so it is guilty of theft and must pay back double to the depositor.

Bank Records

A warehouse owner will keep an inventory of everything stored in his warehouse. He records the identity and contact details of the owner of each item. He can transfer the ownership to another person, if instructed to do so by the original owner. However, this recording system will be separate from his asset register.

Banks should be doing the same thing. They should be keeping an inventory of all the money being stored and the identity of its owners. This should be separate from their financial accounts. The money stored should not creep onto the bank's balance sheet.

Bailment

Bailment is an important legal concept. It is the process of placing personal property in the temporary custody or control of another person. The custodian of the property is responsible for the safekeeping and return of the property. For a bailment to be valid, they must have actual physical control of the property. They are not entitled to the use of the property while it is in their possession, and the owner can demand to have the property returned at any time.

The main feature of a bailment is that possession of the property transfers to the custodian, but ownership is unchanged. A bailment does not transfer ownership. Trusting my furniture to a warehousing company for storage is a bailment. The warehouse has possession of my furniture, but ownership remains with me.

The second feature of a bailment is that the custodian is not entitled to use the property for their own purpose. The warehouse company is not entitled to use my furniture. If a deposit in a cheque account were a bailment, then the bank could not record the money as an asset on its balance sheet. It could not lend it out.

Several decisions by British Law Lords during the nineteenth century established the principle that a demand deposit at a bank is not a bailment. In a case in 1811, Sir William Grant ruled that money paid into a bank is not a bailment, but a loan. The banker is not a bailee, but a debtor (Carr v Carr). In a subsequent case, he said, "The money paid into a banker immediately becomes a part of his general assets and he is merely a creditor for the amount" (Devayne v Noble). In 1844, Lord Cottenham summed up these decisions.

> Money, when paid into a bank, ceases altogether to be the money of the principal; it is then the money of the banker, who is bound to an equivalent by paying a similar sum to that deposited with him when he is asked for it. The money placed in the custody of a banker is, to all intents and purposes, the money of the banker, to do with it as he pleases; he is guilty of no breach of trust in employing it; (Foley v. Hill).

This was a really bad decision for bank depositors, but it has been blindly accepted all over the world ever since. According to modern law, a bank deposit is not a bailment, so the bank is entitled to record the deposit as an asset on its balance sheet.

Honest Money

God dislikes dishonest money. The Instructions for Economic Life have a key principle.

> If a man gives his neighbour silver or goods for safekeeping and they are stolen from the neighbour's house, the thief, if he is caught, must pay back double. But if the thief is not found, the owner of the house must appear before the

judges to determine whether he has laid his hands on the
other man's property (Ex 22:7-8).

When someone takes the goods of another for safekeeping and they
go missing, they are accountable for the loss. If the thief is found,
the thief is responsible. If not, the person caring for the property
is accountable. Their neglect is the same as theft.

This passage describes the valuables presented for safekeeping
as the "property" of the depositor, even when they are in the house
of the other person. This confirms the principle that the ownership
of property does not transfer to a person who takes it for
safekeeping. The owner of the property remains the owner until
the goods are actually sold. This is a bailment.

Applying this principle to banking, the bank that treats money
that has been deposited for safekeeping as its own asset has
misappropriated something that does not belong to it. It has "laid
its hands on the other man's property". If it were taken before the
judges, it would have to pay back double to the owner.

Torn Donkey

There are limits on the duty of care. The person providing
safekeeping is not accountable for events beyond their control.

> If a man gives a donkey, an ox, a sheep or any other animal
> to his neighbour for safekeeping and it dies or is injured or
> is taken away while no one is looking, the issue between
> them will be settled by the taking of an oath before the Lord
> that the neighbour did not lay hands on the other person's
> property. The owner is to accept this, and no restitution is
> required. But if the animal was stolen from the neighbour,
> he must make restitution to the owner. If it was torn to
> pieces by a wild animal, he shall bring in the remains as
> evidence and he will not be required to pay for the torn
> animal (Ex 22:10-13).

The principle remains the same. The owner is the owner. The
neighbour providing care is never the owner. If the animal is stolen,
the neighbour must make restitution to the owner. If the animal is
killed by wild animals, the neighbour does not have to make
restitution, because this event was beyond their control.

The same applies to a bank. If it claims money that has been deposited as its own asset, it has committed theft. If the bank is robbed, it must make restitution to the depositor. However, if the money is destroyed by a fire or war, the bank is not liable for the loss, because it was beyond the bank's control. A bank must provide the best care possible for money deposited, but it is not accountable for events beyond its control.

Creating Credit

The incorrect accounting method used by banks gives them the power to create unlimited credit. This is a serious problem for any economy.

Anyone can create credit. If I supply you with goods or services and say that you can pay me in a year's time, I have created credit. However, I can only give away stuff that I do not need until next year, so there is a serious limit on how much credit I can create. I have to give up something that I own but do not need.

Businesses can create credit, too. If a business supplies goods or services to a person or another business and agrees that no payment is required until three months later, it has created credit. This credit becomes money because the buyer can use the money they would have paid to the business to buy something else.

However, a business has a constraint on the amount of credit that it can create. The credit created will be relatively small, because most of its resources will be used to keep the business operating. A businesses balance sheet looks like this.

Assets	Liabilities
Cash at Bank	
Inventories	
	Loans
Capital Equipment	
Land and Buildings	Owners Equity

Additional credit will need to be funded from equity or by additional borrowing (loans). This significantly limits the amount of credit a business can give.

Assets   Liabilities

Cash at	Debtors
Invento	
Capital Equipment	
Land and Buildings	

| Loans |
| Owners Equity |

Banks create credit too. However, the structure of a bank's balance sheets means that it is not constrained in the same way as other businesses. Banking regulations specify that banks must keep enough reserves to cover potential withdrawals of deposits. Deposit insurance means that their reserves can be quite small. A banks balance sheet looks like this.

Assets   Liabilities

| Loans |
| Currency |
| Reserves |

| Deposits |
| Owners Equity |

When making a loan, the bank places a deposit in their client's account. It records this deposit as a liability on its balance sheet. The mortgage is recorded on the other side of the balance sheet as an asset. The balance sheet is larger but still in balance.

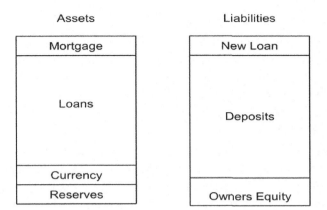

Banks Get the Money Back

Banks are different from other businesses, as most of the money that they lend comes back to them. The bank deposits the money in the account of the person taking out the mortgage. It will not stay there, because the borrower will write a cheque to pay for a house that they are buying. The house seller will deposit the cheque in their bank account, sometimes in a different bank.

The seller will use some of the money to pay for goods and services. They might buy some shares or units in a superannuation fund. The money will be deposited in the banks of the businesses selling these things. Whatever the person does, the borrowed money will be deposited in an account at a bank.

The credit created by the bank issuing the mortgage could be paid into an account at a different bank. However, other banks will be making loan transactions at the same time. The homebuyer's bank would receive money paid into the accounts of parties to these transactions. If all the transactions cancelled each other out, the bank would receive back all the money that it has loaned.

Every day, banks will be writing loans and receiving deposits. All credit created will be matched with a deposit at another bank in the banking system. In practice, some banks would gain extra deposits and others would end up with less. One bank will be up on one day and others will be up on other days. The banks can easily sort out these differences at the end of the day by making payments using the interbank settlement process (usually by adjusting reserves at the central bank).

Banks are different from other businesses, because the credit they create comes back. When a business gives credit to a customer, they hand over goods or services to them. They do not get anything back until the loan is due. Money does not come back into their business.

In contrast, banks do not lose anything when giving credit to a borrower, because the credit created always comes back into the banking system when sellers deposit the payments they have received. When all banks are lending, they have the ability to create immense amounts of credit.

Banks simultaneously create credit and debt. This credit creation has been a major cause of instability in economies everywhere. Created credit often flows into property booms and speculation on the share market. This creation of credit could not happen if deposits were treated as a bailment. If banks stopped recording money deposits as an asset in their accounts, the unlimited creation of credit would not be possible.

False Assumptions

People assume that central banks create money, but that is not correct. In a modern economy, most money is in the form of bank deposits, and these deposits are created by the banks themselves. The amount of new money is equal to the amount of new lending by banks. Banking regulations permit it, but it is the banks who create the credit.

Economics textbooks say that banks receive deposits and lend them out. The assumption is that households and businesses determine the level of lending by deciding how much to deposit with banks. This is not correct. The process is the other way around. Banks create money. Whenever a bank makes a loan, it simultaneously creates a deposit in the borrower's bank account, which becomes new money. When this is used to buy something, it becomes a deposit in the seller's account.

The other common misconception is that central banks limit the volume of loans by controlling the amount of central bank money and fixing a reserve ratio (money multiplier approach). Modern central-bank practice is to target interest rates instead of controlling reserve ratios, so a "money multiplier" no longer applies.

Limits on Bank Credit

Although modern banking regulations give banks the ability to create credit, several factors limit how much they can create.

- A bank needs to find customers wanting to borrow. Central banks determine interest rates. The demand for loans at the official rate will be limited. If the central bank raises interest rates, the numbers of borrowers will decline. If it lowers interest rates, the demand for loans will increase. The amount of credit that banks can create at the rate set by the central bank will be limited.

- Banks have to keep their lending profitable. If they reduce their interest rate to lend more, it might be unprofitable.

- A bank cannot get out of line with what other banks are doing. If it is creating credit and the others are not, then most of the deposits would go to other banks. Settling the shortfall would put pressure on the bank's reserves.

- Banks will need to ensure their capital and reserves comply with relevant regulations, but these are usually quite lax.

The ability of banks to create credit resulted in the massive burden of debt described in chapter 8. In the world system, people, families, businesses and governments are all weighed down by debt.

Economic Stability

Banks make economies unstable by creating too much credit. Excessive mortgage lending feeds into frequent property booms and busts. When people get over-confident and bid up property prices, the banks facilitate their exuberance by funding it with created credit.

Speculative bubbles begin with demand motivated by over-confidence and greed. However, an increase in the price of land or shares due to extra demand does not increase the money supply. It simply shifts purchasing power to those who own the desired assets and away from those whose assets have declined in popularity. The boom cannot expand further unless the banking system provides more credit to finance additional purchases at higher prices.

The ability of banks to create credit exaggerates the effects of greed by fuelling the demand for speculative goods. But credit creation works two ways. When confidence fails, the credit created by the banks is liquidated quickly, causing the economy to collapse.

In God's economy, where love and sharing are more important than covetousness and greed, instability should not be a major problem. There will be times when the economy will expand due to new technology, increased confidence, the discovery of mineral resources, or good weather conditions. However, once better banking has been established, the growth will not be exaggerated by banks creating credit.

From time to time, producers will make mistakes and get the mix of investment and consumer goods wrong. However, the resulting surplus or shortage will quickly clear when prices adjust. The recession will not be exaggerated by the implosion of credit created by banks.

Better Solution
People use banks for two different purposes.

- Recording half-completed transactions while they are waiting for the opportunity to spend. They want to pay for things they need for daily life when they need them.
- Saving money that they do not need now for use in the future. Some will want interest to compensate them for giving up the use of their money for a time.

Banks attempt to provide a service that confuses these needs. The next chapter outlines a way to record half-completed transactions that does not need government power and is consistent with God's Instructions for Economic Life. Chapter 18 describes a better way to manage savings.

17

Obligation Recording

God's Economy needs better money and better banks. Change could happen in two ways:

- Under pressure from consumers, existing banks could offer a contract that does not give them ownership of the money deposited. If people chose the banks with a better contract, others would be forced to match them.
- The existing banking systems might collapse under stress, and wise people who are ready for the opportunity could develop a better process in their place.

The first option is not likely to occur, because too many people would lose too much power. This chapter explains how a better buying and selling process could emerge within Kingdom Communities and be offered as a service to the people of the world.

The following parable describes a transaction-recording process very simply to give readers a clear understanding of its core elements. It is a parable, not a prescription. Practical implementations will need to be more complex, but the underlying principles will be the same.

A Parable

Once upon a time, a small kingdom had no money system. All trade had to be conducted by barter. This lack limited the growth of the economy. The king wanted to encourage trade. He could have decreed that a rare commodity be used as money, but being a wise king, he did nothing and waited.

One day, a wise man, with a reputation for honesty, was sitting at the gate of the kingdom. A group of people who had been exchanging goods with each other fell into dispute. The wise man saw an opportunity and offered to investigate. He tracked down and recorded all the trades that had taken place between them. Once his list was complete, it became obvious that one person had received more than he was entitled to and another had gone short. When the information was presented to them, the person who had received too much agreed to give it back to the one who had missed out.

The wise man saw an opportunity and suggested that for a small fee, he would begin recording all transactions. This action would reduce the risk of fraud. His idea was well received because people would benefit from better information about the prices at which goods were trading.

The wise man recorded all transactions in a book. When a person sold some wool to another person for three units, the clerk would record +3 beside their name and -3 by the person's name. The first person could then go and buy a slab of butter from someone else for one unit, 1 would be deducted from their record, and 1 would be added to the other's record.

The wise man did not set prices. The price was always agreed between the two people trading. People could look at the list of trades that had already taken place to determine what their goods or services were worth. The first trades would be for commonly traded goods and services (like bread or a daily wage for a labourer), so people could estimate the value of their good or services in terms of the unit being used.

When a major food producer began to accept the wise man's records, his system really took off. People were happy to trade using his recording system because they knew they could always get value in food.

At the end of each day, a full set of transactions may not have been completed. In the clerk's book, some people would have a positive record and others would have a negative record. However, the sum of positive and negative records would be equal, as every time someone was recorded as selling something, someone else would be recorded as having bought it.

The value of outstanding transactions would vary enormously from day to day. Some days most people would have completed their transactions, so the total value of outstanding transactions would be quite small. On other days when a lot of people were in the market, the outstanding balances might be quite large. However, this would not matter, because the total value of positive records would always be matched by equivalent negative records.

A problem would occur if people who had nothing to sell ran up a negative record. To prevent this from occurring, the wise men would require people with negative records to clear them within a few days. If they didn't get back to zero in that time, the clerk could refuse to record their transactions. Most people would not risk this happening, because it would prevent them buying and selling.

People without a reputation would only be allowed to go positive, which would mean they would always have to sell something before they could buy. People with good reputations would have the choice of buying first or selling first, depending on what was convenient for them.

This system would allow trade to develop rapidly. The only limitation would be that trade could only take place in the place where the clerk could record it. The wise man would eventually take on other clerks to assist him by doing the same task at different places in the city. This expansion would allow trade to expand further.

At the end of each day, the clerks would get together to sort out their records. Some of the clerks would have a positive total in their book and the others would be negative. A clerk would be up one day and down on another, depending on where trade took place on a particular day. The differences would not matter because the total records across all the clerks would balance to zero. The records in the books of the clerks are not their assets; they are just a record of transactions that have occurred.

In practice, several clerks might set up as transaction-recorders. If the first clerk was not serving an area properly, another person with an honest reputation might see an opportunity to start a similar business. This would not matter as long as all clerks recorded transactions accurately and continued to net off their balances at the end of the day.

Having a choice of clerks would benefit the people, as if one started being dishonest, they could punish him by switching their business to another. This risk would be a strong incentive for the clerks to remain honest. The clerks would watch each other and if one is dishonest, the others would refuse to work with him. This would drive him out of business. Provided the people trusted the clerks to remain honest, the economy would have increasing trade.

The clerks could improve their service by using computers to record transactions. They would provide telephone links to shops and businesses so that they could record transactions directly without visiting a clerk. The clerks could also set up booths around the city where people could do transactions. The kingdom would then have a fully functioning money system to facilitate trade. There would be no need for the king to create money and control it.

Opportunity

Providing sound money is a big opportunity for God's people. The money systems of the world are shaking and may eventually collapse. If that happens, some Kingdom Communities could start a community-based transaction-recording service as an alternative to failing banks.

A banking system is an information network recording claims and obligations. These change as people buy and sell goods and services. The body of Jesus is a network of relationships, so it could be the basis for a transaction-recording network.

A person trusted by everyone within a Kingdom Community could start keeping records on behalf of the people that belong to it. They would offer a community-based service by recording transactions for people within their neighbourhood buying and selling from each other. Once the service is widely accepted, it could be offered to everyone in the neighbourhood.

When people see that others trust the process and that this way of doing business offers greater flexibility in buying and selling, more people will decide to participate in the record-keeping service. The trusted person could expand their activity by providing the same service for other Kingdom Communities.

By recording transactions, the honest person could build up a record for everyone in the neighbourhood. The next step would be for a person who has received something from another to settle their debt by asking the record-keeper to reflect this transaction on their system. The buyer's record would be decreased and the record for the person supplying the goods increased. A trusted record-keeper could facilitate trade within the neighbourhood by adjusting the records of people as they exchange goods and services.

Multiple Recorders

Although the first mover has an advantage, several people might begin a transaction-recording service in the same area. Many transactions would be between clients of the different transaction-recorders, but this is not a problem. A person with a positive record with one transaction-recorder will get them to reduce it and get another transaction-recorder to increase the record of the person who has supplied them with goods or services by the same amount.

A transaction-recorder would be happy to pass a positive record to another recorder because it does not belong to them, but to the person they recorded it for. They would not mind if the person who was previously positive went negative in their records, because it is not a debt owed to them, but an obligation to the rest of the community.

When a transfer is made between transaction-recorders, one recorder has simply reduced the value recorded for one of their clients. They do not have fewer assets, because the claims recorded are not their assets. The other recorder increases the value for one of its clients. It does not have more assets, as the claim is owned by the client. Their solvency is not affected.

The negative and positive records of a particular record-keeper will no longer balance. One might have negative records exceeding positives and another might have positives exceeding negatives. Who records an obligation does not matter, as long as it is recorded somewhere.

The records of all transaction-recorders will still balance. They are just recorded by different transaction-recorders. For everyone in the community who is owed something, there would be another person in the community who owes the same amount. If all the records were combined together, positive and negative records should cancel out across the entire system.

Other Communities

The people keeping records for their Kingdom Community could establish links with people doing the same task in other communities. Record-keepers will be able to transfer records to other record-keepers because they are not shifting value, but simply transferring positive or negative records. When someone completes half a transaction, it does not matter who records it, provided it is recorded by someone trustworthy.

Some transaction-recorders will establish links with recorders in other nations. Apostles would use their networks to develop these links. These transaction-recorders would develop processes for long-distance payments. Merchants managed these types of transactions long before the emergence of modern banking by providing letters of credit that are really just a positive record. A network of linked relationships will support the transfers needed to support international trade and international giving.

Recording Business

To illustrate the process clearly, I have referred to the transaction-recorder as a person. Initially, this person could be someone who produces things that everyone in the community needs or an elder who is trusted by everyone in the Kingdom Community. However, a transaction-recorders will eventually grow into a business organisation with branches in several communities.

If the business grew, a small fee could be charged for the recording service. Most people should be willing to pay for the service they are receiving.

Pay to everyone what you owe them (Rom 13:7).

At first, record communication would be simple and manual. As trading expanded, the record-keepers would develop electronic systems. They would eventually develop a distributed and mobile system that can record transactions anywhere in the community. This would be a fully functioning payment system. Provided transaction-recorders have good backup systems, computer records will be a secure way to record them

I continue to refer to these businesses as transaction-recorders, rather than banks, because this makes their role clearer. Modern banks undertake a similar role, except that they record the transactions as their own assets and liabilities, which is wrong. Transaction-recorders merely record the commitments of the community and obligations to it.

Recording Obligations

The task of a transaction-recording service is to keep a record of people who are owed something by the community and those who owe something to it. These records facilitate buying and selling. In a barter transaction, two people give and receive at the same time. The transactions are reciprocal, so there is no outstanding obligation. With selling and buying, the giving and receiving are not reciprocal. After the first half of a sales transaction:

- The seller has given but has not received.
- The buyer has received but has not given.

The buyer has taken on an obligation to give something to someone in the community. Often, they will have had a previous obligation from the community wiped out.

The seller is entitled to receive something from someone in the community who has a surplus they want to sell. More likely, they will have had a previous obligation to supply something to someone in the community wiped out.

A positive record is evidence that something of value has been provided to someone in the community, while a negative record indicates that the person has received more from their community than they have delivered. The negative record is a commitment to deliver something to someone in the community in the near future.

The commitment of the community to someone with a positive record is quite weak. People with positive records hope that they can find something they want from someone willing to sell at a price they agree to. Usually, they will already have seen something they wish to buy offered for an acceptable price. However, if no one agrees to sell at the price they are willing to pay, they cannot demand that the leaders of the community force someone to sell to them.

The obligation to the community of the person with a negative record is much stronger. If they refuse to clear their record by selling something for a reasonable price, they are stealing. If they don't return what they bought or sell something of similar value to someone in the community, a judge could convict them of theft. If they refuse to make the specified restitution, they could be prevented from buying and selling.

Community

The usefulness of a transaction-recording service is created by the community that trusts it. Transaction-records represent a commitment by the community. The right to receive goods in return for a positive record is personal, residing with the person who holds it, but the obligation to provide the goods or services in exchange rests with the entire community.

When a person buys something from someone from outside the community, they commit the community to selling something to them if they can agree to a price covered by their positive record. That person can choose who they will buy from and what they will buy, provided they can agree on a price with the seller. They are free to choose the person offering the best price.

When people accept a positive record with the transaction-recording service, they are trusting other people in their community to accept it in exchange for goods or services. They do not have to trust everyone in the community, but they will need to know there are enough trustworthy people in the community to give the community-based process credibility. They also need to know that the transaction-recorders in the community can be trusted.

The value of positive records on the transaction-recording service depends on the people of the community honouring their obligations. There is a strong biblical basis for respecting a community-based recording service.

> Pay to everyone what you owe them... Let no obligation
> remain outstanding, except the continuing obligation to love
> one another (Rom 13:7-8).

The people of a Kingdom Community should honour and respect the community-based transaction-recording process

The leaders of a community will want to protect the reputation of their community. They will meet the obligations of their community themselves by supplying something to a person with a positive record, if no one else does. The stronger the community, the greater will be the trust in their transaction-recording service.

Trust will be important when getting the transaction-recording process started. However, once the process is operating, trust becomes less important because people can see goods and services be offered in exchange for positive records all around them in the market. They will give up what they have in exchange for a positive record because they can see numerous businesses offering something in exchange for it.

Unit

A transaction-recording service records incomplete transactions. The unit that claims and obligations are recorded in does not matter, provided everyone understands and uses it. It can relate to a particular commodity or to a currency that has existed in the past. People can look at the price of goods and services offered for sale to decide what it is worth.

The unit does not have value. Buyers use it to express the value they see in what they are buying when they agree to a price. Sellers will look at what other people are offering for what they want when deciding how much they are willing to accept for their product.

Rules

Transaction-recorders will apply the Instructions for Economic Life by protecting people who have completed half-transactions from theft. Each community will decide the rules of operation for their recording process. Most of these rules will be applied automatically by the transaction-recording process.

- Only people who are known and trusted within the community will be able to go negative. They are not being given credit, because they are already creditable. Rather, their honesty and reliability are being recognised.
- A person who is not trusted by the community can join the transaction-recording process, provided they sell before they buy. Once they have a positive record, they can be trusted for that amount. The process rules would prevent them from going negative until they have established their reliability by selling and buying a number of times.
- If an untrustworthy person is poor, they can join the payments process if someone from the community gives them an interest-free loan to get started. The loan will be

personal debt between the giver and receiver because no one has the authority to make a loan on behalf of the community.

- Negative records must be cleared within a few days by selling something to someone in the community.
- People who do not redeem their negative records will be automatically blocked from buying. They will not be able to sell until they return to a positive record. If the person is poor with nothing to sell, they might need a member of the community to give them a poor-loan so they can survive.
- The size of negative records will be capped. They are not a problem in themselves, because they represent an obligation to the community to provide goods or services in the future. However, the size of negative records will be limited to minimise the temptation to buy something and then scarper.
- A negative record not redeemed within the required time frame should be treated as a theft. Judges could specify a penalty of fourfold restitution if there are no extenuating circumstances. If the person refuses to make restitution, they could be excluded from community activities.
- The size of positive records will also be capped. Big positive records are a problem because insiders will be tempted to cheat the system and steal them. A cap on the size of positive records will minimise the risk of theft.
- People wanting to make a big, expensive purchase would not be allowed to go negative for a large amount. They would need a positive record of sufficient value before buying. They could get this by saving or getting a loan through a loan-organiser (see chapter 18).
- Most prices will be public so that everyone can see what things are worth. Some large transactions will be confidential to protect the privacy of buyers and sellers.
- Transaction-recorders will open their records to anyone who wants to audit their activity.
- Transaction-recorders must not treat positive records as an asset they own. They must not be recorded as an asset on their balance sheet.

- Transaction-recorders must not lend positive records to people or businesses who might want them. They do not have authority to lend them to someone else. If a transaction-recorder lent them, then two people would be planning to spend the same positive record, which is wrong.
- Transaction-recorders must not pay interest on positive records.
- The only way that positive records can be available for lending is if the owner agrees not to use their positive record for a specific time. That makes it available to be lent to someone for the same time period. If people decide to lend their positive record, it must be done formally, so that it remains clear who has the right to spend (see chapter 18).
- Transaction-recording to facilitate selling and buying must be kept separate from saving and lending.

Transaction-recorders will regularly review their rules to ensure they are effective and not unnecessarily penalising people.

I have described transaction-recorders as people, but once the process is functioning effectively, it should be mostly automated. Once the operating rules are agreed, the transaction-recording process would implement them automatically.

Monitoring Recorders

The transaction-recording process will be largely self-policing. If a recorder lost trust, people would quickly shift their business to a different recorder. Transaction-recorders would watch each other carefully. If one could expose another making illegitimate transactions, it could eliminate a competitor and increase market share. People would transfer their records to honest recorders, and the dishonest one would go out of business.

If transaction-recorders transfer money that belongs to one person to another without permission, the victim should charge it with theft. If convicted of theft, the judges could require the transaction-recorder to make double restitution to those whom it had defrauded. This restitution would be a double punishment, as the negative publicity would most likely destroy their business.

The various transaction-recorders in a community would be competing with each other to be trusted. To sustain their business, they would have to prove to their customers that their records were accurate. They would need to open their records and processes to external monitoring to demonstrate their reliability. They would have to open their records up to anyone who wanted to check.

Most people would not have time, so specialised monitors could undertake the task. They could check the transaction-recording process ensure the records net to zero. This check would quickly expose any fraud. Record-monitoring businesses could support the community by publishing their findings.

Monitors would also check that transaction-recording businesses are not treating the positive records of their customers as their own assets. Monitors would charge transaction-recorders shifting positive records to their balance sheet with theft.

Portable Records

Some transaction-recorders could issue paper vouchers as a service to their society. The voucher would enable the holder to buy goods or services from anyone who trusts the transaction-recording process. The recipient could hand the voucher back to the money-recorder and get a positive record in exchange. Or they could hand it to someone else in exchange for goods or services.

When a person gets a voucher from a transaction-recorder, it will subtract from their record an amount equivalent to the voucher issued. It will not increase the account of someone else as would happen with normal buying and selling. An electronic record of a claim has just been replaced with a paper record. Nothing else has changed. The total value of claims would still net to zero, provided the value of the paper vouchers are included in the calculation.

No Government

Governments have no role in the transaction-recording process. The volume of claims outstanding is not something that a government needs to control. Nor should it be kept constant, or only allowed to increase at a constant rate. The volume of positive records that exists at any time will depend on how many people have completed both their buying and selling.

It is possible, in theory, that at the end of the financial year, all people will have completed all their transactions. If there are no outstanding half-completed transactions, the total volume of claims would be zero. In practice, this is unlikely to occur, as in the modern economy the flow of transactions from sellers to buyers is continuous. However, the fact that it is theoretically possible for all positive records to be extinguished at a particular time makes controlling the volume of outstanding records unwise. It can be small on one day and large a few days later, depending on how people stream their transactions.

A government cannot create a money-recording service, because its viability depends on the trust of the people and businesses in the community. It will only be trusted for buying and selling if other businesses are willing to supply goods and services in exchange for positive records.

A common assumption is that state money is trusted because the government mandates it, but this is not correct. A government cannot make its money valuable. It cannot force people to trust the money it has created. All a government can do is demand payment of taxes in legal tender. This creates some demand for the state money, but it does not establish trust in it.

People will only accept state money if they see people and businesses accepting it in exchange for goods and services. If trust disappeared, people will stop using government money and find other ways to trade. A government cannot prevent that from happening. If businesses stop accepting state money in exchange for goods or services, its value disappears, regardless of the laws behind it.

Trust in a transaction-recording service is created by a community. It does not need the authorisation of a king or government. Positive records are trusted because the people of the community accept them in exchange for goods and services.

Persecution Proof

If Christian individuals and churches hold their money in the world's banking system, the government can easily confiscate it. A transaction-recording service based within a Kingdom Community will be much safer. If the government began accessing the computers of the transaction-recording services they could narrow their recording down to people they trust. If necessary, they could even shift back to recording transactions on paper or in a notebook. This would allow followers of Jesus to continue trading with each other despite the persecution.

Records of the obligations of the community have no value outside the community. If the government stole the records, people in the community would refuse to acknowledge demands for goods and services in exchange for them. People would ignore positive records that are stolen.

Practical Outworking

I have tried to describe the operation of a transaction-recording service as simply as possible to make the core elements clear. Practical implementations will vary according to the economic and political circumstances, but the underlying principles will be the same. The people of God will have to work out the details by following the leading of the Holy Spirit and adapting the principles to their local situation.

18

Loan-Organisers

Kingdom Communities will encourage transaction-recorders to record the transactions of everyone in their community who is buying and selling. Positive records result from half-completed transactions. They represent the obligation of someone in the community to supply goods and services to the person who has given up something but received nothing in return.

Initially, people will minimise risk by making a purchase quickly to eliminate their positive record. Once they learn to trust the transaction-recorder, some might leave their positive record with the transaction-recorder until they need fresh goods later in the week. Over time, they will want to keep their positive record longer to match the timing of their purchases to their needs.

Savings

When a person receives their wages or salary, they may not need to spend it all in the next fortnight. They might choose to build up their positive record to deal with unexpected problems. If they trust their transaction-recorder, they might want to build up a positive record to make a big purchase in the future.

Building up a big positive record could be sensible for a saver, but it creates a problem for people who have produced things. A positive record sitting with a transaction-recorder is a claim to goods and services. Someone in the economy will have produced them, but will not be able to sell, because the claim to them is sitting with a transaction-recorder. The producer who cannot sell could miss out on income that they need.

The rules of the transaction-recording service will prevent people from building up big positive balances, so a formal process will be needed for people wanting to save for the future. The person wanting to save their positive record would be better to lend it to someone who needs it. The person getting the positive record could agree to pay a fee to compensate them for not using their positive record immediately.

Lending positive records resolves the problem for people who cannot sell things they have produced, because the person getting the loan would be able to buy them. To be able to pay the money back at the end of the term, the borrower would have to forgo some of the goods or services to which they would otherwise be entitled. This means that goods or services will be there for the lender when they get their positive record back.

Loan-Organisers

Organising a loan might be hard if a saver does not know anyone who wants to borrow their positive record. If they do know someone, they might not be sure if they can trust them. Before giving up their positive record for a specific time, they would want to be sure that they could get it back when the term is complete.

People who have successfully lent a positive record might offer to help others to do the same. They would need wide connections and skills to investigate who could be trusted. Once they had been successful in assisting several people to lend, they could establish themselves as a loan-organiser.

Loan-organisers will offer people with positive records an interest payment in exchange for lending them to someone with a need. The borrower would usually be someone needing productive equipment or to build up their trading stocks. The loan-organiser would check their trustworthiness before making the loan.

Loan-organisers must be trustworthy people. Some will have established trust as an elder in their Kingdom Community. Others will have confirmed their reliability by serving as deacons using gifts of money to provide interest-free loans to the poor.

A transaction-recorder should probably not become a loan-organiser, as they would lose their independence and people might stop trusting them. Trust is so important to their business that they would need to avoid any activity that would put it at risk.

Modern banking systems get transaction-recording and loan organising mixed up. Most bank deposits can be withdrawn on call, but the bank lends the money deposited for a fixed term. This practice is dangerous because if everyone decides to withdraw their money at the same time, the bank could fail. Keeping these two activities separate prevents this from happening.

Loan-Organiser's Role

Savings, lending and borrowing link the present and the future, so trust is essential. Loan-organisers establish trust between savers and borrowers. Their role includes the following tasks.

- They will pool savings with the same term into a fund that can be loaned to borrowers.

- A loan-organiser will choose between the various people who want to borrow. They will take into account the potential of the loan to advance the Kingdom of God.

- They would assess the risk of potential borrowers. Links with elders in other Kingdom Communities will be useful when making these assessments.

- They will work closely with transaction-recorders to implement the transaction. When the loan is made, they will instruct the transaction-recorder to adjust the records of the lenders and the borrower to reflect the loan of the savings.

- The positive record of the saver will be reduced by the amount of the loan. This prevents them from using the money that they have saved until the agreed term is complete.

- The record of the borrower will be increased by the same amount. This enables them to buy the goods they have taken a loan to purchase.

- The loan-organiser will ensure that a contract with the saver is agreed. It will specify the term and the conditions under which their savings can be lent.
- They will get the contract with the borrower agreed. It will specify the term and the interest that will be paid for the loan.
- The loan-organiser might obtain insurance to cover the risk of borrowers defaulting.
- Loan-organisers will love their neighbours by negotiating agreements that are good for both lenders and borrowers.
- The maximum term for a loan will be seven years.

A loan-organiser could begin as one person but would usually be a business organisation. I call them "loan-organisers" so that their role is clear. They are not banks in the modern sense, because they do not own the money that savers place with them. They organise loans between savers and borrowers, but they do not record savings on their balance sheets.

Linking Lenders and Borrowers

All loans should have a fixed term. The owner of the positive record agrees not to use it for a specified time in return for interest. The person taking the loan commits to building up their own positive balance and returning it at the end of the loan term.

Loan-organisers will match the savings of people who want to save to the needs of people who want to borrow. Each loan must be matched savings with the same term. The interest rates for various terms will be adjusted so that the supply of savings matches the demand for loans for each term.

The loan-organiser will charge a flat fee or a margin on the interest rate to cover the cost of their service. They would assess the credit-worthiness of potential borrowers and the viability of the projects for which they are borrowing. The loan-organiser might also agree to take responsibility for any bad debt. The cost of this service would be included in their fee.

Re-financing loans is part of the loan-organiser's role. If a lender's situation changes and they need the money they have loaned, they may need to withdraw it early. As it has been lent for a fixed term, early repayment would have to be renegotiated.

The loan-organiser should be able to replace the money with a loan from another saver, but the person withdrawing their savings would have to pay the cost. The market interest rate may have fallen, so the first lender may also have to cover the difference for the rest of the term. However, the cost should be small, as in a sound financial system interest rates will be quite stable.

Matched Loans

Two principles are essential for honest lending.

- All loans would be for a fixed term.
- Every loan will be matched by savings with the same term.

These principles are incredibly simple, but they are the key to sound banking. They ensure that whenever someone borrows a claim to goods or services, there is someone else willing to give up an equivalent claim to goods and services at the same time.

Loan-organisers cannot create credit. They can only lend savings that have been assigned to them by others for lending. Every loan issued by the loan-organiser must be matched by a savings or pool of savings with the same term. They can only make a loan if savers have committed to making matching savings.

The modern banking system depends on lending and borrowing that does not match. Most residential mortgages have a term of 15 to 20 years, but much of the funding comes from term deposits with a term of a year or less. Borrowing money short-term for lending long-term is unwise because banks are promising money they do not have for periods in the future. They just hope that they will be able to obtain it when they need it.

During a time of uncertainty, people could panic and many could try to withdraw their savings at the same time. If the bank cannot call up all its loans, it could run out of reserves. A run could push the bank into bankruptcy and many people would lose their money. Bank panics have been common throughout the history of banking.

Matching loans and savings is safer because loan-organisers will know that borrowers will be repaying their loan when the term comes to maturity. The loan-organiser will know where the money that belongs to the savers has gone and when it will be coming back. This would eliminate a significant part of the risk.

Matching the terms of savings and loans will reduce financial instability. The interest rate for matched loans might be lower, but the risk would be lower as well. Insisting on matching loans would cause interest rates on longer-term loans to rise. This is reasonable, as the longer the term of the loan, the greater the risk of loss.

In the Kingdom of God, all loans should be short-term. We should not make contracts which unnecessarily bind our future. The Instructions for Economic Life suggest the maximum time that we can bind ourselves is seven years (Deut 15:1). Committing to repay a loan in twenty or thirty years' time is very unwise, so very long-term loans will disappear.

Risk of Default

Matching the term of the loan to the term of the saving does not eliminate all risk. People can get into financial difficulty, despite their best intentions. Some people are dishonest, some are greedy and anyone can be tempted if the opportunity arises. The person who borrowed the money might make bad business decisions and lose it. These uncertainties mean that lending money to another person is always risky.

Loan-organisers will attempt to identify honest borrowers who will be willing and able to repay the loan when its term is complete. They should be skilled in assessing the creditworthiness of borrowers and setting the interest rate appropriately. The interest received should be sufficient to compensate the saver for the risk.

The money paid for the hire covers the loss (Ex 22:15).

Every transaction that involves the future has uncertainty, so despite the efforts of loan-organisers, risk is unavoidable. Savers will choose the level of risk they are willing to bear. If a borrower's venture is risky, the interest rate will be higher to compensate. Safer investments will pay a lower rate. Most savers will specify that their money is only lent to creditworthy borrowers. Some savers will want a higher rate of return and will be willing to take on greater risk to obtain it. The loan-organiser will inform savers about various options available and the risks involved and let them choose what is right for them.

A loan-organiser might offer insurance to cover the risk of borrowers defaulting in return for a slightly lower interest rate. This does not eliminate all risk, but it spreads the cost across numerous savers, rather than leaving all the risk with the few savers affected by the bad loan. Many savers will accept a lower interest rate if they know that the cost of any default is being shared with other savers.

In the Kingdom Economy, dishonesty should be less common. If borrowers are walking in the Spirit, their ventures should be successful. Therefore, the margin added to the interest rate to cover risk should be quite small.

Ownership and Risk

Defenders of the modern financial system argue that money in a term deposit belongs to the bank, but this is not correct. When a saver lends to a borrower, the money lent still belongs to the saver. The borrower has been given use of the money for a specified time.

The rules for lending are specified in the Instructions for Economic Life.

> If a man borrows an animal from his neighbour and it is injured or dies while the owner is not present, he must make restitution. But if the owner is with the animal, the borrower will not have to pay. If the animal was hired, the money paid for the hire covers the loss (Ex 22:14-15).

When an animal is borrowed by a neighbour, it remains the property of the owner. The owner is still the owner.

Although the animal was lent for a fee or lease, the neighbour is required to take reasonable care. However, if something unexpected goes wrong, then he does not have to pay compensation. The lease fee will have included a margin to cover the risk of the animal dying. The owner has to carry the risk.

These principles apply to savings lent for a fixed term. The person who lends their savings still owns the money. Therefore, loan-organisers should not record savings available for lending as an asset on their balance sheet.

Lending and borrowing are different from transaction-recording. A transaction-recording service provides a safe-keeping service in the same way as a warehouse. A positive record can be spent whenever the owner chooses. A loan is different because although the saver still owns the money, they have lent their positive record to another person for a specific time. They cannot demand their money back at any time but must wait until the end of the agreed term. Ownership is not transferred, but permission to use the money is transferred to the borrower for a specific time.

Kingdom of God
Followers of Jesus will often produce more than they consume. They will make their savings available to loan-organisers who are committed to advancing the Kingdom of God.

- Loan-organisers connected to a Kingdom Community will lend to projects that will strengthen the relationships within the community.
- They will support business activities that strengthen the relationships between Kingdom Communities.
- They will support businesses that grow food for people who are hungry and to provide food and shelter for people in need.
- They will support businesses that provide employment within the Kingdom Community.

19
Investment-Organisers

Economic development comes as people enhance their efforts using productive equipment. All productive assets originate with someone saving. Savings are channelled into productive equipment in two main ways.

- Loans to businesses who want additional equipment.
- Investing in businesses that need to buy productive equipment.

Debt can be dangerous, so as the Kingdom of God grows, dependence on debt will decline. Savers will channel their saving into productive assets by investing in businesses that are expanding their activities.

Investment-Organisers

When people and business escape from debt, the volume of debt will shrink significantly. Loan-organisers will find that opportunities for lending savings have dried up. Some will develop a role helping people channel their savings into productive businesses. Investment-organisers have two roles.

- Search – seeking out new investment opportunities.
- Stewardship - to watch over existing investments to protect and enhance the value of their client's asset.

Modern banks have mostly failed to do these tasks. Instead, they channel savings into property and speculative financial products.

Investment-organisers will assist people to pool their savings and invest in businesses that need extra resources to grow. The savers will buy a share in the equity of businesses that need more productive equipment.

Investment-organisers will encourage savers to invest in businesses that provide employment and strengthen their Kingdom Communities.

Managing Risk

Helping investors to understand and manage risk is an essential part of the investment-organiser's role.

Investment-organisers will assess the businesses requiring funds to ensure they are viable. They will help investors understand the riskiness of the business.

- Risk is unavoidable, so investors will need to be alert. Even if the investment potential is investigated thoroughly by an investment-organiser, a business can make a mistake and lose money.
- The managers of the businesses seeking funds will ensure that the risks are well understood.
- The lines of intermediation will be short. Investment-organisers will link savers with investors.
- Investment-organisers will allow savers to decide the degree of risk they want to carry. Some people may be willing to take higher risk for better returns. This would assist businesses developing new ideas to get funds.

The massive expansion of packaging, repackaging and trading of existing assets that created the risk causing the global financial crisis will come to an end.

Investment Funds

Some investment-organisers will establish funds to hold a variety of business assets. This would enable savers to spread their risk by buying shares in one of these funds. Investment-managers would give them a legal structure in which the investors jointly own the assets and receive a share of returns in proportion to their investment. Investment funds will function in the following way.

- All funding would be obtained by expanding the share-holding. New funds will be used to buy new business assets.
- The managers of the fund do not own the assets held by the fund. They are jointly owned by the investors in the fund in proportion to their contribution.
- The investors in a fund share the risk, so there will be no need for Investment-managers to put up capital to cover risk.
- If a fund is wound up, investors will receive a share of the sale of the assets in proportion to their contribution.
- Investors will usually withdraw their savings by selling their shares. The price will be determined by market demand.
- The managers of investment funds will be careful people, not flashy big-spenders. They will be responsible for stewarding the assets on behalf of the investors. They should not be speculating with investors funds for their own benefits.
- The investment-organisers who manage investment funds will take a fee for their services. Fees will be set in a way that minimises incentives to buy speculative financial assets.
- Investment funds will avoid debt. This will eliminate the problems of leverage that plagues modern financial markets.
- The managers of the organisations will specify clearly the range of assets they are buying. This will enable investors to choose companies that matched their appetite for risks.
- Different investment funds will provide savers with the types of investments. Some will prefer long-term growth, while others might want regular dividends.
- Some investment funds will deliberately support businesses starting new activities or engaged in innovation. These investments will involve more risk, but some savers will be willing to take greater risks for the long-term benefit of their community.
- Some funds will support businesses that need a large-scale operation to be efficient.
- Investment funds will focus on the long-term growth of their communities, rather than short-term profits.

- Funds will minimise risk by diversifying their assets as much as possible. Managers will attempt to choose assets that respond differently to changed economic situations so that if one declines in value others might compensate.
- In an uncertain world, risk cannot be eliminated. Investment-organisers will make risk as transparent as possible.
- Investment funds will avoid speculative activities with borrowed money as this will produce unrighteous wealth.
- Investment funds should aim to own real businesses with real productive assets. They will avoid the synthetic financial products created by bankers and lawyers that are disconnected from real business assets as these are a significant cause of booms and busts. They will stay away from the flimsy superstructure of financial derivatives that has been built on top of the modern banking system.
- Investment managers will want to understand the activities of their fund, so they will not let it become too large to control. They will not be seeking power and dominance, so they will not need to be excessively large.

Investment funds will channel savings into productive equipment and other assets that will benefit their economy. They will focus on activities that provide employment and strengthen the relationships within local communities.

20
God's Economy

As the gospel is proclaimed and the Holy Spirit works in human hearts to draw people to Jesus, his Kingdom will spread through the world like yeast in dough. God's Economy will come to fulfilment as his Instructions for Economic Life are implemented.

- God's economy is a good economy. Obeying Jesus is more important than prosperity.
- God's economy will operate without government intervention and control.
- Economic behaviour will be shaped by love of neighbour.
- Giving and sharing will be as important as buying and selling.
- Buying and selling will be generous and money will be honest.
- Most people will have enough, and few will have too much.
- Unrighteous wealth will be given away.
- The debt that weighs on society will collapse and disappear.
- Everyone will have sufficient land for their needs.
- Employers will help their staff find work that utilises their gifts and gives them fulfilment.
- Employees will be paid sufficient to live on
- When nationalism disappears, the military-industrial complex that dominates modern economies will fade away.
- God's creation will be restored from frustration.

Radical Change

These are radical changes, but the Holy Spirit can achieve them because he is willing to start small and grow by multiplication. All he needs is groups of people committed to loving each other and willing to trust and obey him to establish a Kingdom Community.

Jesus said the Kingdom of God is like a mustard seed (Mark 4:31-32). When a tiny mustard seed is planted it appears as a small twig, but its branches grow rapidly and multiply quickly until in a few years it has become a tall tree with spreading branches.

A kingdom is not one person obeying a king, it is a place where all the people are ruled by a king. Each manifestation of the Kingdom of God will begin small in a village, or city street or block when a small group of people decide to live there in close vicinity to each other. As they tell the good news, heal the sick, share their possessions and give away their unrighteous wealth, many of their neighbours will be drawn to Jesus.

The followers of Jesus in a place become a Kingdom Community when they commit to providing justice, protection and social support for everyone living in that place, whether or not they follow Jesus. Kingdom Communities will grow and multiply in the same way as the mustard seedling grows by sending out shoots that quickly mature into strong branches.

Starting with small groups of people serving each other in Kingdom Communities, the Holy Spirit will prompt them to send the best people out as apostles to repeat the process in another place. Kingdom Communities will join together in prayer to squeeze the spiritual powers of evil out of the territory of their king.

When the people living within each Kingdom Community apply God's Instructions for Economic Life, the rich will give away their unrighteous wealth. The poor will be blessed as their debts are cancelled. The humble will be lifted up as Jesus promised. As followers of Jesus love one another and apply the Instructions for Economic Life, God's Economy will emerge in the place where they live.

About the Author

Ron McKenzie is a Christian writer
living in Christchurch, New Zealand.
During the 1980s, he served as
the pastor of a church,
but found that he did not fit that task.
He was employed as an economist
but has recently retired from his role.
He is married with three adult children
and several grandchildren.

Made in the USA
Middletown, DE
13 February 2022

61059115R00116